W9-AHH-829

History Alive!®
The Ancient World

TCi™

Chief Executive Officer
Bert Bower

Chief Operating Officer
Amy Larson

Director of Product Development
Maria Favata

Strategic Product Manager
Nathan Wellborne

Social Studies Team Manager
Ginger Wu

Senior Editor
Mikaila Garfinkel

Program Editors and Writers
Sally Isaacs
Lauren Kent
Beth Lasser
Tylar Pendgraft
Alex White

Production Manager
Jodi Forrest

Operations & Software Manager
Marsha Ifurung

Senior Production Designer
Sarah Osentowski

Art Direction
Julia Foug

Teachers' Curriculum Institute

PO Box 1327

Rancho Cordova, CA 95741

Customer Service: 800-497-6138

www.teachtci.com

Copyright © 2017 by Teachers' Curriculum Institute.

Permission is granted to reproduce student materials for classroom use only.

Printed in the United States of America.

ISBN 978-1-58371-218-4

5 6 7 8 9 – SIN – 23 22 21 20 19

Manufactured by Sinclair Printing, Palmdale, CA
United States of America, July 2019, Job 1902504

Acknowledgments

Program Author
Wendy Frey

Contributing Writers
John Bergez
Mark Falstein
Diane Hart
Marisa A. Howard
Amy Joseph

Curriculum Developers
Joyce Bartky
April Bennett
Nicole Boylan
Terry Coburn
Julie Cremin
Erin Fry
Amy George
Jake Kerman
Anne Maloney
Steve Seely
Kelly Shafsky
Nathan Wellborne
Alex White
Ginger Wu

Reading Specialist
Kate Kinsella, Ed.D
Reading and TESOL Specialist
San Francisco State University

Teacher Consultants
Melissa Aubuchon
Indian Trail Middle School
Plainfield, Illinois

Anthony Braxton
Cruickshank Middle School
Merced, California

Amy George
Weston Middle School
Weston, Massachusetts

Randi Gibson
Stanford Middle School
Long Beach, California

Lisa Macurak
New Windsor Middle School
New Windsor, Maryland

Sherry Owens
Lubbock Independent School
District
Lubbock, Texas

Acknowledgments

Scholars

Dr. Anthony Bulloch
University of California, Berkeley

Dr. Mark W. Chavalas
University of Wisconsin, La Crosse

Dr. Eun Mi Cho
California State University, Sacramento

Dr. Steve Farmer
Palo Alto, California

Dr. Bruce Grelle
California State University, Chico

Dr. David N. Keightley
University of California, Berkeley

Dr. Brij Khare
California State University, San Bernardino

Dr. Richard Klein
Stanford University

Dr. John W.I. Lee
University of California, Santa Barbara

Dr. Kate McCarthy
California State University, Chico

Dr. Gary Miles
University of California, Santa Cruz

Dr. Daniel Veidlinger
California State University, Chico

Dr. Jed Wyrick
California State University, Chico

Dr. Joel Zimbelman
California State University, Chico

Assessment Consultants

Denny Chandler
Curriculum and Assessment Specialist
Cold Spring, Kentucky

Julie Weiss
Curriculum and Assessment Specialist
Elliot, Maine

Music Consultant

Melanie Pinkert
Music Faculty
Montgomery College, Maryland

Cartographer

Mapping Specialists
Madison, Wisconsin

Internet Consultant

Amy George
Weston, Massachusetts

Diverse Needs Consultants

Erin Fry
Glendora, California

Colleen Guccione
Naperville, Illinois

Cathy Hix
Swanson Middle School
Arlington, Virginia

Unit 1
Early Humans and the Rise of Civilization

Geography Challenge 2

Chapter 1: Investigating the Past 5

Chapter 2: Early Hominins 11

Chapter 3: From Hunters and Gatherers to Farmers 17

Chapter 4: The Rise of Sumerian City-States 23

Chapter 5: Ancient Sumer 31

Chapter 6: Exploring Four Empires of Mesopotamia 41

Timeline Challenge 47

Unit 2
Ancient Egypt and the Middle East

Geography Challenge 50

Chapter 7: Geography and the Early Settlement of Egypt, Kush, and Canaan 53

Chapter 8: The Ancient Egyptian Pharaohs 59

Chapter 9: Daily Life in Ancient Egypt 67

Chapter 10: The Kingdom of Kush 75

Chapter 11: The Origins of Judaism 81

Chapter 12: Learning About World Religions: Judaism 87

Timeline Challenge 93

Unit 3
Ancient India

Geography Challenge 96

Chapter 13: Geography and the Early Settlement of India 99

Chapter 14: Unlocking the Secrets of Mohenjodaro 105

Chapter 15: Learning About World Religions: Hinduism 111

Chapter 16: Learning About World Religions: Buddhism 117

Chapter 17: The First Unification of India 125

Chapter 18: The Achievements of the Gupta Empire 129

Timeline Challenge 135

Unit 4
Ancient China

Geography Challenge   138

Chapter 19: Geography and the Early Settlement of China   141

Chapter 20: The Shang Dynasty   147

Chapter 21: Three Chinese Philosophies   153

Chapter 22: The First Emperor of China   159

Chapter 23: The Han Dynasty   167

Chapter 24: The Silk Road   173

Timeline Challenge   181

Unit 5
Ancient Greece

Geography Challenge   184

Chapter 25: Geography and the Settlement of Greece   187

Chapter 26: The Rise of Democracy   191

Chapter 27: Life in Two City-States: Athens and Sparta   197

Chapter 28: Fighting the Greco-Persian Wars   205

Chapter 29: The Golden Age of Athens   211

Chapter 30: Alexander the Great and His Empire   219

Chapter 31: The Legacy of Ancient Greece   225

Timeline Challenge   231

Unit 6
Ancient Rome

Geography Challenge   234

Chapter 32: Geography and the Early Development of Rome   237

Chapter 33: The Rise of the Roman Republic   241

Chapter 34: From Republic to Empire   245

Chapter 35: Daily Life in the Roman Empire   251

Chapter 36: The Origins and Spread of Christianity   259

Chapter 37: Learning About World Religions: Christianity   265

Chapter 38: The Legacy of Rome in the Modern World   269

Timeline Challenge   277

Credits   279

Early Humans and the Rise of Civilization

Geography Challenge

Lesson 1: Investigating the Past
How do social scientists interpret the past?

Lesson 2: Early Hominins
What capabilities helped hominins survive?

Lesson 3: From Hunters and Gatherers to Farmers
How did the development of agriculture change daily life in the Neolithic Age?

Lesson 4: The Rise of Sumerian City-States
How did geographic challenges lead to the rise of city-states in Mesopotamia?

Lesson 5: Ancient Sumer
Why do historians classify ancient Sumer as a civilization?

Lesson 6: Exploring Four Empires of Mesopotamia
What were the most important achievements of the Mesopotamian empires?

Timeline Challenge

North Africa and the Middle East

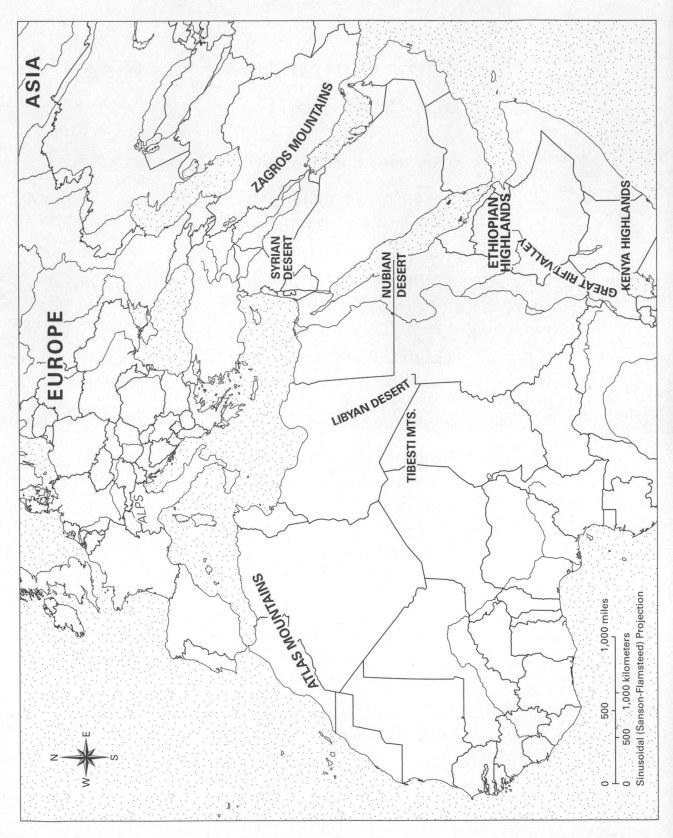

© Teachers' Curriculum Institute

Geography Skills

Analyze the maps in "Setting the Stage" for Unit 1 in the Student Text. Then answer the following questions and fill out the map as directed.

1. Locate the continent of Africa on the outline map. Label it. Which continent lies to the north of Africa? Which continent lies to the northeast of Africa?

2. Locate the Nile River and label it on your map. Into which body of water does the Nile River flow?

3. Locate the Nile River valley. Shade and label it on your map.

4. What is the Fertile Crescent?

   Locate the Fertile Crescent on your map. Shade and label it. Which river(s) runs through the Fertile Crescent?

5. Label the body of water off the west coasts of Europe and Africa. Also label the bodies of water off the east and north coasts of Africa.

6. Check the map in the Unit 1 "Setting the Stage" in the Student Text to find an early human fossil discovery that was made in the Great Rift Valley. On your outline map, use an X to mark the location of that discovery.

7. Label the Sahara and the Arabian Desert on your map. Then circle the following features: Syrian Desert, Nubian Desert, Libyan Desert.

8. Most of the land of North Africa and the Middle East is desert. How did this affect the settlement of early people?

Critical Thinking

Answer the following questions in complete sentences.

9. Considering the geographical physical features, why do you think early humans migrated eastward to the Fertile Crescent, rather than north to Europe?

10. One region in the Middle East is called Mesopotamia. This name means "the land between the rivers." Where do you think this region lies?

11. The Fertile Crescent was made up mostly of grassy plains. While this area was good for farming, it lacked resources such as stone, wood, and metal. What hardships might these shortages have caused for the people who lived there?

12. Why did most early civilizations develop near a water supply?

© Teachers' Curriculum Institute

Investigating the Past

How do social scientists interpret the past?

In the space below, quickly sketch one object that you currently own and that you think someone might find 20,000 years from now.

Suppose that you are a social scientist living 20,000 years from now. You have just discovered the object above. What might the object tell you about the person who left it behind? Write your thoughts in a short paragraph below.

Social Studies Vocabulary

As you complete the Reading Notes, use these terms in your answers.

archaeologist	geographer	prehistoric
historian	artifact	ritual

1. Complete the matrix below to compare three types of social scientists.

	Archaeologists	Historians	Geographers
What do they do?			
What questions do they ask?			
Symbol for their work			

2. In a complete sentence, answer the following question: *How are social scientists like detectives?*

1. List three things social scientists can learn from cave paintings.

2. Sketch and label two artifacts that have been found in caves.

   © Teachers' Curriculum Institute

Section 3

1. Before reading, label three details in the image that may offer clues about why the artist created this painting.

2. Write a hypothesis stating why you think the artist created this painting.

3. Read Section 3. Label any additional important items in the image.

4. Why do social scientists think this painting was created?

Section 4

1. Before reading, label two details in the image that may offer clues about why the artist created this painting.

2. Write a hypothesis stating why you think the artist created this painting.

3. Read Section 4. Label any additional important items in the image.

4. Why do social scientists think this painting was created?

Section 5

1. Before reading, label three details in the image that may offer clues about why the artist created this painting.

2. Write a hypothesis stating why you think the artist created this painting.

3. Read Section 5. Label any additional important items in the image.

4. Why do social scientists think this painting was created?

Section 6

1. Before reading, label two details in the image that may offer clues about why the artist created this tool.

2. Write a hypothesis stating why you think the artist created this tool.

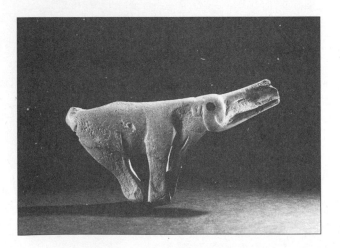

3. Read Section 6. Label any additional important items in the image.

4. Why do social scientists think this tool was created?

© Teachers' Curriculum Institute

Section 7

1. Before reading, label two details in the image that may offer clues about why the artist created this sculpture.

2. Write a hypothesis stating why you think the artist created this sculpture.

3. Read Section 7. Label any additional important items in the image.

4. Why do social scientists think this sculpture was created?

Section 8

1. Before reading, label two details in the image that may offer clues about why the artist created these tools.

2. Write a hypothesis stating what you think the artist did with these tools.

3. Read Section 8. Label any additional important items in the image

4. What do social scientists think these tools were used for?

PROCESSING

Social scientists learn about the past by asking questions and conducting inquiries. You can be a "history detective" too!

What is something that you wonder about the past? You might wonder why an event happened or how something got to be the way it is today. Write your question below.

My compelling question: _____

_____

Now plan an inquiry to answer your question.

- Think of one specific question each of the social scientists below might ask. These questions should help answer your bigger, compelling question.
- Brainstorm sources where you could find information to answer these supporting questions.

	Supporting Questions	Sources of Information
Archaeologist		
Historian		
Geographer		

                                   © Teachers' Curriculum Institute

Early Hominins

What capabilities helped hominins survive?

PREVIEW

Think of your favorite superhero from a comic strip, book, or movie. In the space below, sketch a simple picture of your superhero and write his or her name.

List two or three capabilities your superhero has. In complete sentences, explain why these capabilities are important.

© Teachers' Curriculum Institute

READING NOTES

Social Studies Vocabulary

As you complete the Reading Notes, use these terms in your answers.

hominin   capability

anthropologist   migrate

Section 1

1. In the spaces below, write the scientific name of this hominin. Then list any other nicknames for this hominin group.

 _ _ _ _ _   _ _ _ _ _ _ _

2. Color the rectangle that matches the time period in which this hominin lived.

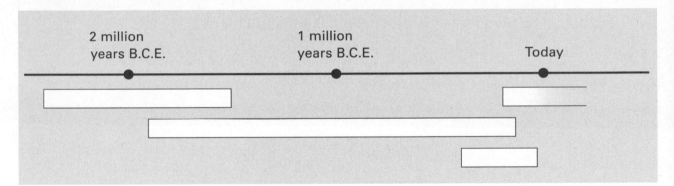

2 million years B.C.E.   1 million years B.C.E.   Today

3. In the image, color or draw the key capabilities of this hominin. Label each one.

4. Explain why each capability you labeled was important for survival. Include the following terms in your explanation: *groups, tools*.

          © Teachers' Curriculum Institute

1. In the spaces below, write the scientific name of this hominin. Then list any other nicknames for this hominin group.

_ _ _ _   _ _ _ _ _ _ _ _

2. Color the rectangle that matches the time period in which this hominin lived.

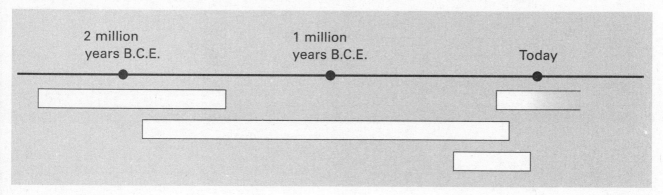

2 million
years B.C.E.

1 million
years B.C.E.

Today

3. In the image, color or draw the key capabilities of this hominin. Label each one.

4. Explain why each capability you labeled was important for survival. Include the following terms in your explanation: *strong bones, fire, shelter.*

© Teachers' Curriculum Institute

Section 3

1. In the spaces below, write the scientific name of this hominin. Then list any other nicknames for this hominin group.

 _ _ _ _   _ _ _ _ _ _ _ _ _ _ _ _ _ _ _ _ _

2. Color the rectangle that matches the time period in which this hominin lived.

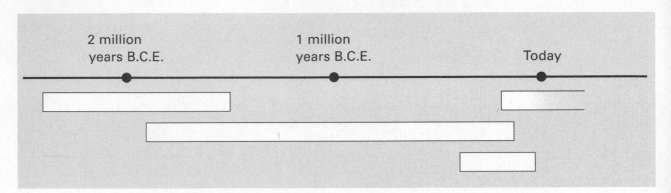

3. In the image, color or draw the key capabilities of this hominin. Label each one.

4. Explain why each capability you labeled was important for survival. Include the following terms in your explanation: *groups, spears, community.*

   © Teachers' Curriculum Institute

1. In the spaces below, write the scientific name of this hominin. Then list any other nicknames for this hominin group.

— — — —   — — — — — — —

2. Color the rectangle that matches the time period in which this hominin lived.

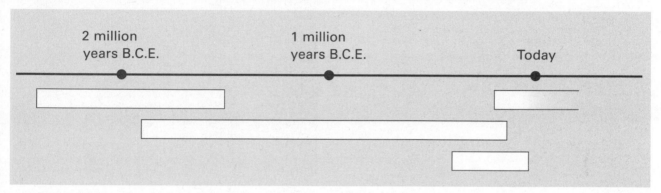

2 million years B.C.E.   1 million years B.C.E.   Today

3. In the image, color or draw the key capabilities of this hominin. Label each one.

4. Explain why each capability you labeled was important for survival. Include the following terms in your explanation: *tools, clothing, weapons, artwork.*

PROCESSING

Create a fact-filled "superhero" poster for the hominin group you found most interesting. The poster should focus on the capabilities of the hominin you select. Your poster needs to include

- the scientific name and nickname of your hominin.
- information about where and when your hominin lived.
- a drawing of your hominin group doing something in their natural environment.
- a description of your hominin's important capabilities.
- any other creative ideas that make the poster more visually appealing.

© Teachers' Curriculum Institute

From Hunters and Gatherers to Farmers

How did the development of agriculture change daily life in the Neolithic Age?

In the boxes below, create a two-part cartoon strip that shows one way that the invention of the computer changed people's lives. Use simple drawings to show what the people in the cartoon are thinking or saying.

In the Past	Today

READING NOTES

Social Studies Vocabulary

As you complete the Reading Notes, use these terms in your answers.

Paleolithic Age	Fertile Crescent	domesticate	nomad	resource
Neolithic Age	Catal Hoyuk	agriculture	trade	

Section 1

1. Briefly describe what life was like in the Paleolithic Age and the Neolithic Age.

2. Where were many Neolithic settlements located and why?

Section 2

1. How did people obtain food in the Paleolithic Age? What were some of the problems with obtaining food this way?

2. Answer each question by filling in the speech bubbles for Neolithic Nel. One example is done for you below.

Rather than gather wild plants, what did Neolithic people learn to do?

We learned that we could grow our own food by collecting and planting the seeds of plants.

What did Neolithic people learn about domesticating animals?

What is agriculture? Why was the invention of agriculture important?

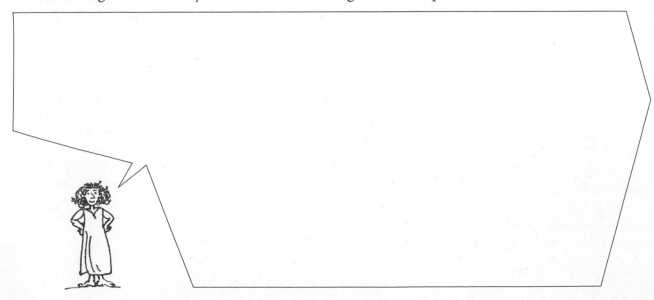

© Teachers' Curriculum Institute

Section 3

1. What did people use for shelter in the Paleolithic Age? Why were these shelters temporary?

2. Answer each question by filling in the speech bubbles for Neolithic Nick.

How were houses built in the Neolithic Age?

How did Neolithic people use their houses to store and cook food?

Why was the development of permanent shelters important?

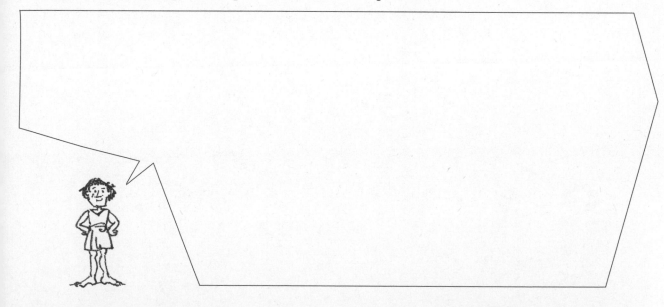

© Teachers' Curriculum Institute

Section 4

1. Why were communities small during Paleolithic times?

2. Answer each question by filling in the speech bubbles for Neolithic Nel.

How did community living help Neolithic people become better organized?

What advantage did Neolithic people get from working together in communities?

Why was the establishment of communities important?

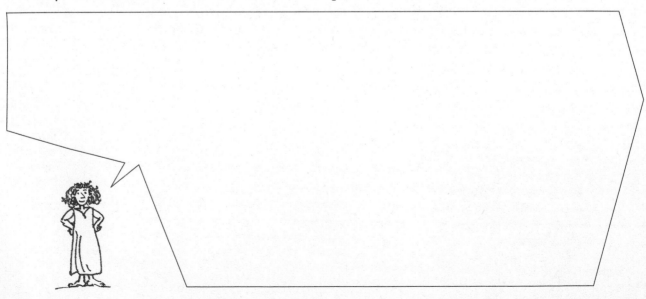

© Teachers' Curriculum Institute

Section 5

1. What was the most important job in the lives of Paleolithic people?

2. Answer each question by filling in the speech bubbles for Neolithic Nick.

What were some of the specialized jobs of the townspeople of Catal Hoyuk?

Why did Neolithic people decorate pottery and polish stones?

Why was the development of different jobs important?

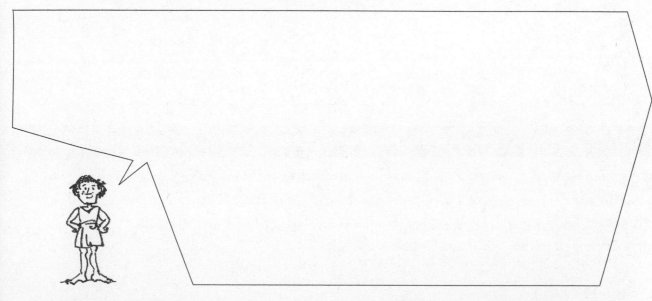

© Teachers' Curriculum Institute

1. What resources did Paleolithic people use?

2. Answer each question by filling in the speech bubbles for Neolithic Nel.

Why did Neolithic people trade?

How did Neolithic people conduct trade?

Why was the growth of trade important?

PROCESSING

On a separate sheet of paper, write a paragraph answering the Essential Question:

How did the development of agriculture change daily life in the Neolithic Age?

Compare and contrast how people got their food, where they lived, and the skills they developed in the Paleolithic and Neolithic ages.

© Teachers' Curriculum Institute

The Rise of Sumerian City-States

How did geographic challenges lead to the rise of city-states in Mesopotamia?

Think of a recent problem or challenge that you faced, and what you did to solve it. In the "Problem" box in the flowchart below, draw a simple illustration of the problem or challenge. Also in that box, write a one-sentence summary of the problem. In the "Solution" box, draw a simple illustration to show how you solved the problem. Also write one sentence describing the solution.

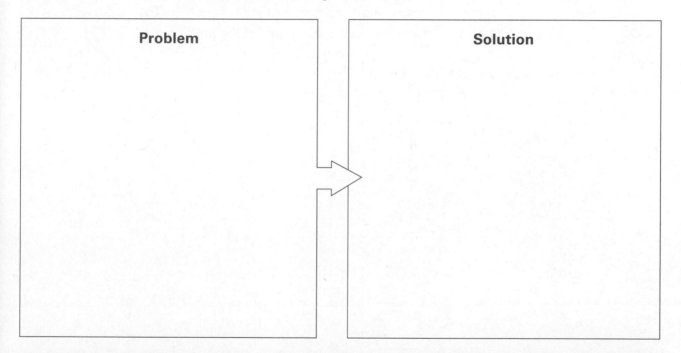

Problem	Solution

Social Studies Vocabulary

As you complete the Reading Notes, use these terms in your answers.

Mesopotamia	Euphrates River	irrigation	silt
Tigris River	Sumer	levee	city-state

List five words or phrases that characterize the geography of Mesopotamia. Circle
the one characteristic that might pose the biggest challenge to people living there.
In a complete sentence, explain why you chose this characteristic.

Section 2

1. What were some advantages of living in the foothills of the Zagros Mountains?

2. In the "Problem" box, draw and label a simple picture showing the problem that occurred around
   5000 B.C.E. Also in that box, write a one sentence summary of the problem.

   In the "Solution" box, draw a simple illustration to show how the farmers in the foothills solved
   the problem. Also write one sentence describing the solution.

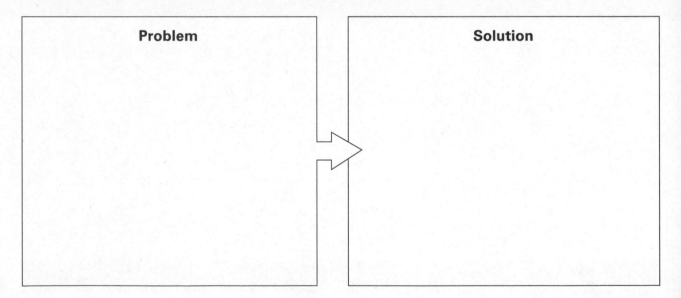

Problem	Solution

3. Who were the Sumerians?

© Teachers' Curriculum Institute

Section 3

1. Describe the seasonal weather changes in Sumer.

2. In the "Problem" box, draw and label a simple picture showing the problem
   caused by an uncontrolled water supply. Also in that box, write a one sentence
   summary of the problem.

   In the "Solution" box, draw a simple illustration to show how the Sumerians
   solved the problem. Also write one sentence describing the solution.

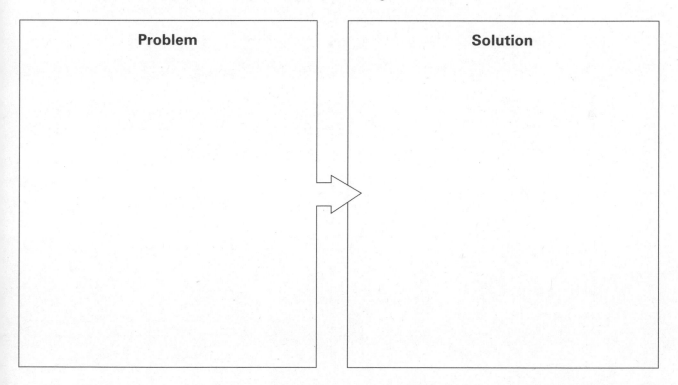

| **Problem** | **Solution** |

3. In what other ways did the Sumerians control the water supply?

1. What new problem occurred after Sumerian farmers created irrigation systems?

2. In the "Problem" box, draw and label a simple picture showing the problem that could happen to an irrigation system that was not maintained. Also in that box, write a one sentence summary of the problem.

In the "Solution" box, draw a simple illustration to show how the Sumerians solved the problem. Also write one sentence describing the solution.

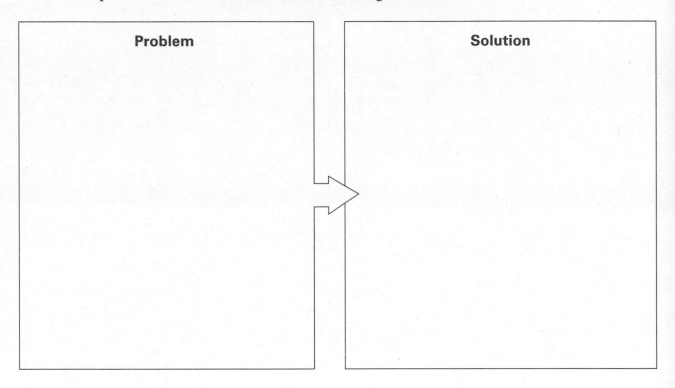

Problem

Solution

3. What was the long-term result of the Sumerians working together?

© Teachers' Curriculum Institute

1. How did the physical geography of Sumer leave its cities unprotected?

2. In the "Problem" box, draw and label a simple picture showing the problem that caused Sumerian cities to fight with each other. Also in that box, write a one sentence summary of the problem.

In the "Solution" box, draw a simple illustration to show how the Sumerians solved the problem. Also write one sentence describing the solution.

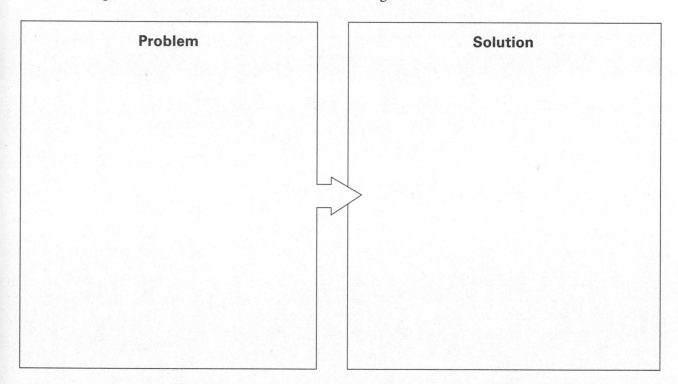

Problem	Solution

3. Why do historians call the cities of Sumer "city-states"?

Section 6

To complete the flowchart, summarize how geography led to the rise of Sumerian city-states. In the appropriate boxes below, list each problem and its solution, as described in the reading.

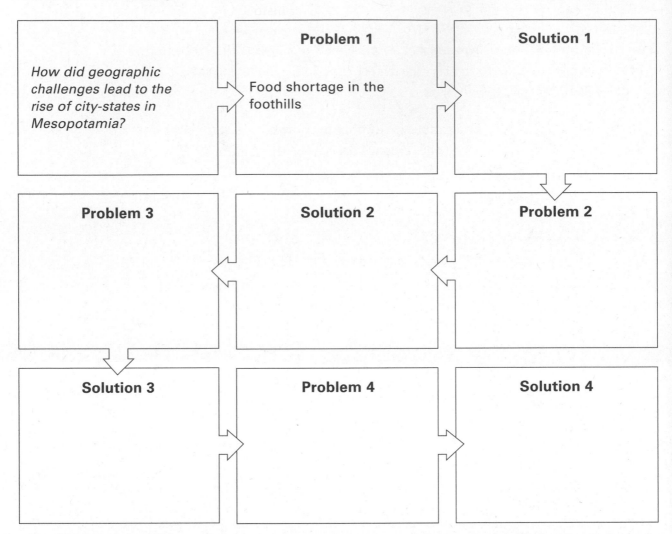

| | **Problem 1** | **Solution 1** |
| *How did geographic challenges lead to the rise of city-states in Mesopotamia?* | Food shortage in the foothills | |

| **Problem 3** | **Solution 2** | **Problem 2** |

| **Solution 3** | **Problem 4** | **Solution 4** |

PROCESSING

On a separate sheet of paper, create a real estate advertisement to encourage people to move to one of the Sumerian city-states. Include the following:

- A clever title for the advertisement, to catch the reader's eye. Be sure it includes the words *Sumerian City-State.*

- At least three illustrations representing the ideas the Sumerians came up with to solve key problems.

- A caption for each visual that describes the solution and why it helped make this Sumerian city-state a desirable place to live.

 © Teachers' Curriculum Institute

Preparing to Write: Analyzing Artifacts

Suppose that you are an archaeologist living five hundred years from now. You are excavating at a site in a flat, deserted area. From reading history books, you know that there was once a big city here. One day, you and your team find the artifact shown below. It is a two-sided coin of some sort. What can you learn from it?

Side 1

Side 2

What five things do you notice about Side 1?

What five things do you notice about Side 2?

Using your observations in the lists above, what are three conclusions you might reach about the unknown society that used this artifact?

Writing to Support a Conclusion

List five personal artifacts found in your bedroom. Then write a paragraph describing one conclusion a future archaeologist might make about you. Use the examples from your list of personal artifacts to support that conclusion. Details about the personal artifacts should strongly support the conclusion.

Use this rubric to evaluate your paragraph. Make changes to your work if you need to.

Score	Description
3	Personal artifacts (details) strongly support the conclusion. The paragraph uses both simple and more complex sentences well. There are no spelling or grammar errors.
2	The paragraph presents a fairly well-constructed conclusion (topic sentence). Personal artifacts (details) mostly support the conclusion. The paragraph uses both simple and more complex sentences fairly well. There are some spelling or grammar errors.
1	The paragraph presents a weakly-constructed conclusion (topic sentence). Personal artifacts (details) do not support the conclusion well. There is little use of more complex sentences. There are many spelling or grammar errors.

© Teachers' Curriculum Institute

Ancient Sumer

Why do historians classify ancient Sumer as a civilization?

Scientists sometimes describe a society or a group of humans as "highly civilized." Explain what you think it means to be highly civilized, and provide specific examples.

Social Studies Vocabulary

As you complete the Reading Notes, use these terms in your answers.

civilization	artisan	cuneiform
social structure	scribe	pictograph
technology	ziggurat	
merchant	culture	

Complete the spoke diagram below. Follow these steps:

1. Write the title of the section in the large center circle.

2. In each small circle, write one of the characteristics of civilization.

3. Next to each small circle, draw a picture or symbol that represents that characteristic.

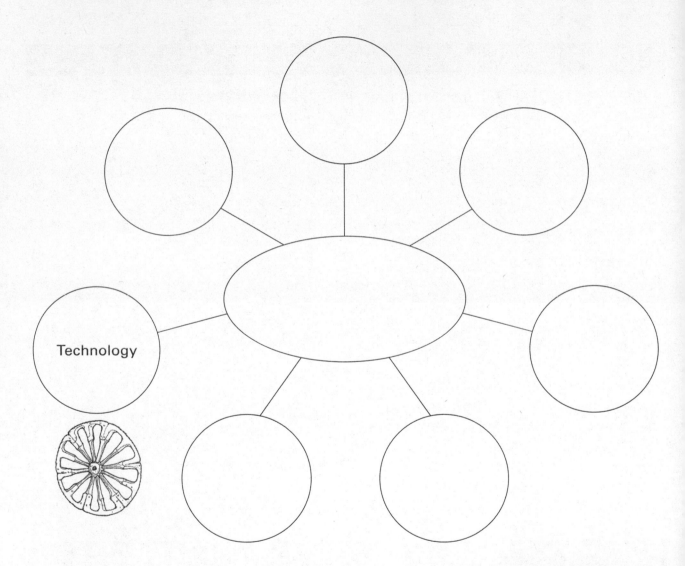

© Teachers' Curriculum Institute

If your class is doing the activity for this lesson, complete all of the Reading Notes for each section. *If your class is not doing the activity, skip the last part of each section.*

Section 2

Complete the flowchart below. In each box, write the name of a Sumerian invention that helped create a stable food supply. Explain what the invention was and how the Sumerians used it.

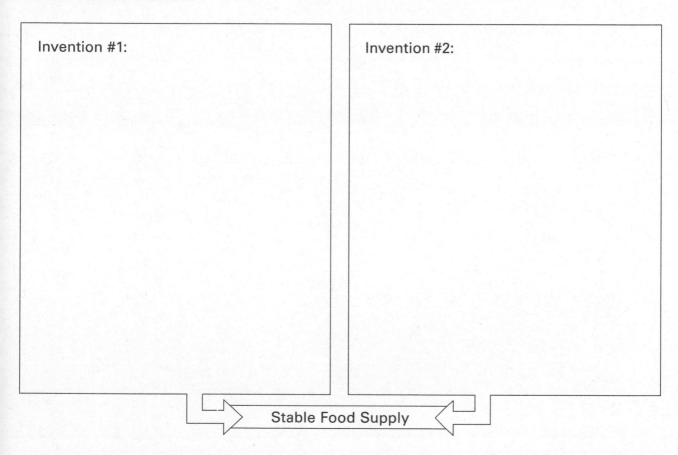

Invention #1:

Invention #2:

Stable Food Supply

(Note: If your class is not doing the activity, skip the following.)

List the artifacts that show evidence of a stable food supply in Sumer. Choose one artifact. Write a sentence explaining how it relates to this characteristic of civilization.

Section 3

In the ladder below, list and describe the people who lived at each status level of the Sumerian social structure. Next to each description, draw a symbol that represents that class.

TOP

MIDDLE

BOTTOM

(Note: If your class is not doing the activity, skip the following.)

List the artifacts that show evidence of social structure in Sumer. Choose one artifact. Write a sentence explaining how it relates to this characteristic of civilization.

  © Teachers' Curriculum Institute

Section 4

Why did religious beliefs in Sumer make the government more powerful?

List all the duties of the government in Sumerian city-states. Circle the duty you think was the most important, and explain why you chose this duty.

(Note: If your class is not doing the activity, skip the following.)

List the artifacts that show evidence of government in Sumer. Choose one artifact. Write a sentence explaining how it relates to this characteristic of civilization.

Section 5

What is a religious system?

Why was religion important in Sumer?

Draw and label a picture that shows two ways Sumerians expressed their religious beliefs.

(Note: If your class is not doing the activity, skip the following.)

List the artifacts that show evidence of religion in Sumer. Choose one artifact. Write a sentence explaining how it relates to this characteristic of civilization.

© Teachers' Curriculum Institute

Section 6

Name three types of artists in Sumer and explain what each one did.

Why was music an important art in Sumer?

(Note: If your class is not doing the activity, skip the following.)

List the artifacts that show evidence of the arts in Sumer. Choose one artifact.
Write a sentence explaining how it relates to this characteristic of civilization.

Section 7

In the flowchart below, draw and label pictures to show what life was like in Sumer
before and after the invention of the wheel.

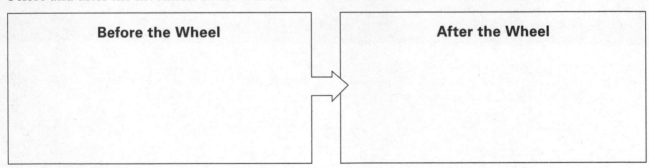

Before the Wheel	**After the Wheel**

Draw and label a picture of a Sumerian arch. Explain why it was an important
technological advance.

(Note: If your class is not doing the activity, skip the following.)

List the artifacts that show evidence of technology in Sumer. Choose one artifact.
Write a sentence explaining how it relates to this characteristic of civilization.

  © Teachers' Curriculum Institute

Section 8

In the flowchart below, explain the development of writing in Sumer, from pictographs to cuneiform.

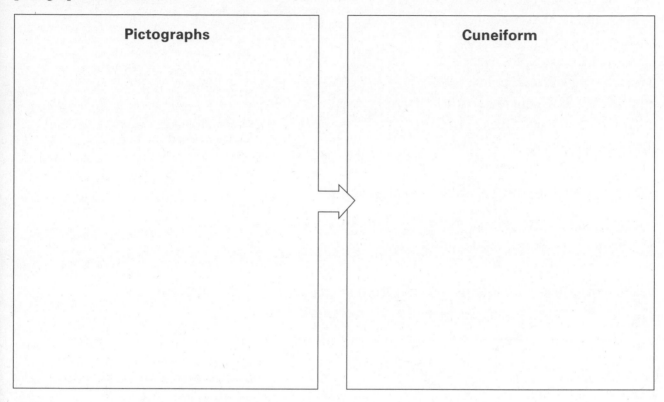

| **Pictographs** | **Cuneiform** |

Why do you think cuneiform was a better method of communication than pictographs?

(Note: If your class is not doing the activity, skip the following.)

List the artifacts that show evidence of written language in Sumer. Choose one artifact. Write a sentence explaining how it relates to this characteristic of civilization.

On a separate sheet of paper, create a spoke diagram as shown here. Find or draw pictures of *modern* items that are examples of each characteristic of civilization. Put the picture next to the characteristic it relates to, and draw a line connecting the picture to the circle.

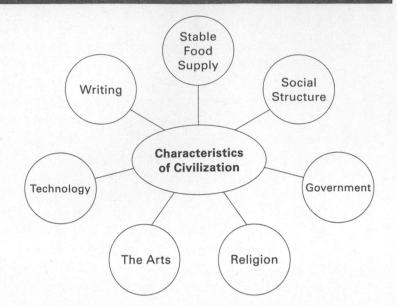

In the table below, list the item you drew for each characteristic of civilization. Then explain how the item relates to that characteristic.

Characteristic	Modern item	How the item relates to the characteristic of civilization
Stable Food Supply		
Social Structure		
Government		
Religion		
The Arts		
Technology		
Writing		

© Teachers' Curriculum Institute

INVESTIGATING PRIMARY SOURCES

Identifying and Evaluating Evidence

Use the reading to create a claim to answer this question: *How did the different social classes of Sumer interact with one another?*

Claim:

What evidence from the primary sources documents support your claim? Fill out the chart below. Circle the two strongest pieces of evidence.

Source	Evidence	How does this support the claim?

You can use this evidence to strengthen your claim. Write your revised claim below.

Constructing an Argument

Create an argument to answer the question: *How did the different social classes of Sumer interact with one another?* Your argument should:

- clearly state your claim.

- include evidence from multiple sources.

- provide explanations for how the sources support the claim.

Use this rubric to evaluate your argument. Make changes as needed.

Score	Description
3	The claim clearly answers the question. The argument uses evidence from two or more primary sources that strongly support the claim. The explanations accurately connect to the evidence and claim.
2	The claim answers the question. The argument uses evidence from one or more primary sources that support the claim. Some of the explanations connect to the evidence and claim.
1	The claim fails to answer the question. The argument lacks evidence from primary sources. Explanations are missing or are unrelated to the evidence and claim.

 © Teachers' Curriculum Institute

Exploring Four Empires of Mesopotamia

What were the most important achievements of the Mesopotamian empires?

In ancient Mesopotamia, rulers recorded their greatest achievements on steles. A *stele* (STEE-lee) is a stone slab on which an illustration or inscription has been carved.

Complete the two steles to celebrate two of your most important personal achievements. Draw pictures or find photographs of images or symbols to represent each achievement.

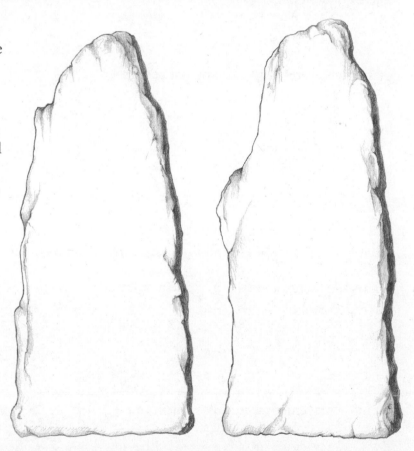

Social Studies Vocabulary

As you complete the Reading Notes, use these terms in your answers.

empire	tribute	economy
capital	code of laws	siege

1. Around what year did the Akkadians conquer the Sumerian city-states? Who was their first leader?

2. In the stele to the right, draw and label pictures to illustrate the *military* achievements of the Akkadian Empire. Then complete these sentences:

   This stele represents the Akkadian military achievement of . . .

   This achievement was important because . . .

1. In the stele to the right, draw and label pictures to illustrate the *cultural* achievements of the Akkadian Empire. Then complete these sentences:

   This stele represents the Akkadian cultural achievement of . . .

   This achievement was important because . . .

2. How long did the Akkadian Empire last? Why did it fall?

© Teachers' Curriculum Institute

Section 3

1. Who was the next king to unite Mesopotamia after the fall
    of the Akkadian Empire, and where was his capital city?

2. In the stele to the right, draw and label pictures to illustrate
    the *political* achievements of the Babylonian Empire. Then
    complete these sentences:

    This stele represents the Babylonian political
    achievement of . . .

    This achievement was important because . . .

Section 4

1. In the stele to the right, draw and label pictures to illustrate the *economic*
    achievements of the Babylonian Empire. Then complete these sentences:

    This stele represents the Babylonian economic
    achievement of . . .

    This achievement was important because . . .

2. What rights did slaves and women have under
    Babylonian law?

Section 5

1. Where was Assyria located? Using the map in the Student Text, describe the areas the Assyrian Empire conquered.

2. In the stele to the right, draw and label pictures to illustrate the *military* achievements of the Assyrian Empire. Then complete these sentences:

    This stele represents the Assyrian military achievement of . . .

    This achievement was important because . . .

Section 6

1. In the stele to the right, draw and label pictures to illustrate the *cultural* achievements of the Assyrian Empire. Then complete these sentences:

    This stele represents the Assyrian cultural achievement of . . .

    This achievement was important because . . .

2. How long did the Assyrian Empire last? Why did it fall?

  © Teachers' Curriculum Institute

Section 7

1. Which group of people regained control of the lands of Mesopotamia after the Assyrians? Who was their most famous king?

2. In the stele to the right, draw and label pictures to illustrate the *military* achievements of the Neo-Babylonian Empire. Then complete these sentences:

   This stele represents the Neo-Babylonian military achievement of . . .

   This achievement was important because . . .

Section 8

1. In the stele to the right, draw and label pictures to illustrate the *cultural* achievements of the Neo-Babylonian Empire. Then complete these sentences:

   This stele represents the Neo-Babylonian cultural achievement of . . .

   This achievement was important because . . .

2 How long did the Neo-Babylonian Empire last? Why did it fall?

PROCESSING

Complete this report card to evaluate the achievements of the Mesopotamian empires you studied. Follow these steps:

- Evaluate each empire's achievements by giving it a letter grade—A, B, C, D, or F—for each category.

- In the comments section, give evidence to support each letter grade you assigned.

Report Card for the Mesopotamian Empires

	Akkadian Empire	Babylonian Empire	Assyrian Empire	Neo-Babylonian Empire
Military and Political Achievements	Grade: Comments:	Grade: Comments:	Grade: Comments:	Grade: Comments:
Economic and Cultural Achievements	Grade: Comments:	Grade: Comments:	Grade: Comments:	Grade: Comments:

© Teachers' Curriculum Institute

Timeline Skills

Analyze the Unit 1 timeline in the Student Text. Also think about what you have learned in this unit. Then answer the following questions.

1. Which hominins lived side by side with prehistoric humans?

2. Which hominins discovered how to use fire?

3. For about how many years did the Neolithic Age last, and why was it important?

4. Where were the world's first cities located, and about when were they established?

5. About when did city-states develop in Sumer?

6. About when did the Sumerians develop cuneiform, and how was it used?

7. Which of these empires—Akkadian, Assyrian, or Babylonian—was the world's first?

8. About how many years after King Hammurabi's reign did the Assyrians establish their empire?

9. Which empire rose to power in Mesopotamia after the Assyrian Empire?

Critical Thinking

Use the timeline and the lessons in the unit to answer the following questions.

10. Describe at least three important differences between life in the Paleolithic Age and life in the Neolithic Age.

11. The majority of the events listed on the timeline occur after 10,000 B.C.E.

    a. How does the work of historians and archaeologists help explain why we know more about recent events than ones that occurred earlier?

    b. How might the development of cuneiform also help explain why we know more about recent events?

12. According to the timeline, how many different empires ruled Mesopotamia between about 2300 and 539 B.C.E.? Identify at least one reason why this region was desirable to conquerors.

13. If you could add two more events to this timeline, which ones would you choose? List each event and explain why you think it is important enough to add to the timeline.

    a.

    b.

© Teachers' Curriculum Institute

Ancient Egypt and the Middle East

Geography Challenge

Lesson 7: Geography and the Early Settlement of Egypt, Kush, and Canaan

How did geography affect early settlement in Egypt, Kush, and Canaan?

Lesson 8: The Ancient Egyptian Pharaohs

What did the pharaohs of ancient Egypt accomplish, and how did they do it?

Lesson 9: Daily Life in Ancient Egypt

How did social class affect daily life in ancient Egypt?

Lesson 10: The Kingdom of Kush

How did location influence the history of Kush?

Lesson 11: The Origins of Judaism

How did Judaism originate and develop?

Lesson 12: Learning About World Religions: Judaism

What were the central teachings of Judaism, and why did they survive to modern day?

Timeline Challenge

Ancient Egypt, Kush, and Israel

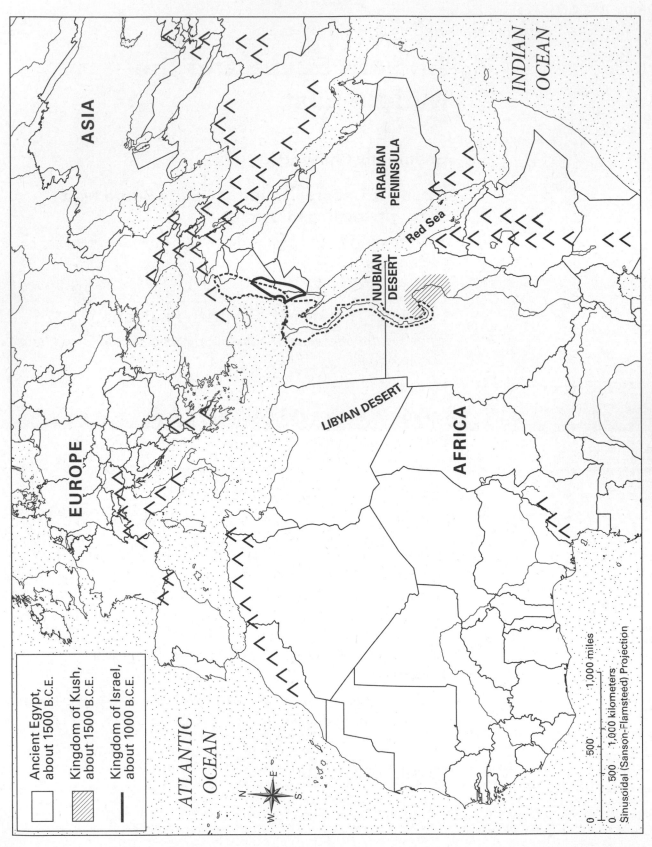

ASIA

INDIAN OCEAN

ARABIAN PENINSULA

Red Sea

NUBIAN DESERT

LIBYAN DESERT

AFRICA

EUROPE

ATLANTIC OCEAN

Ancient Egypt, about 1500 B.C.E.

Kingdom of Kush, about 1500 B.C.E.

Kingdom of Israel, about 1000 B.C.E.

N E W S

1,000 miles

500

500   1,000 kilometers

0

0

Sinusoidal (Sanson-Flamsteed) Projection

© Teachers' Curriculum Institute

Geography Skills

Analyze the maps in "Setting the Stage" for Unit 2 in the Student Text. Then answer the following questions and fill out the map as directed.

1. Locate the Arabian Peninsula on the outline map. Draw a box around it. The Arabian Peninsula is part of which continent?

2. Locate ancient Egypt on the map in the Unit 2 "Setting the Stage" in the Student Text. Shade it on the outline map and key. Egypt is part of which continent?

3. Locate the Nile River and the Nile River delta on your map. Label them.

4. Four large bodies of water touch the shores of the Arabian Peninsula. Locate these bodies of water and label the missing ones on your map.

5. Locate the kingdom of Israel. Label it on your map. Then locate the kingdom of Kush. Label it on your map.

6. Locate the two deserts that surrounded much of ancient Egypt. Circle them on your map.

7. What are the two major vegetation zones in both ancient Egypt and the Middle East?

8. What do the boundaries of ancient Israel tell about its size compared with that of ancient Egypt? Compared with that of ancient Kush?

Critical Thinking

Answer the following questions in complete sentences.

9. Considering the environmental factor of vegetation, why do you think civilization on the African continent began in Egypt, rather than farther west, in central North Africa?

10. What do the locations of deserts, rivers, and seas on this map tell us about where early people were likely to settle?

11. The kingdom of Kush was an important trading center in Africa. Why might its location explain this fact?

12. Ancient Egypt and the Arabian Peninsula have very few mountains. Most of the land is flat, with some low hills in places. How might the geography have influenced what ancient people did to make their living?

13. While most people who lived in ancient Egypt and the Middle East avoided settling in nearby deserts, those regions protected them from their enemies. Why do you think this was true?

14. Ancient Egyptians worshiped the Nile River as a god. Why do you think they did so?

© Teachers' Curriculum Institute

Geography and the Early Settlement of Egypt, Kush, and Canaan

How did geography affect early settlement in Egypt, Kush, and Canaan?

PREVIEW

The environmental factors of an area affect people's choices about where to settle. These factors might include bodies of water, landforms, plant life, and weather.

Examine the landscape drawing that your teacher is displaying. Identify at least three environmental factors that might affect your choice of where to settle. For each factor, explain why it is important. For example, you might write, *The river would provide food and fresh water for my settlement.*

Environmental Factor 1:

Environmental Factor 2:

Environmental Factor 3:

READING NOTES

Social Studies Vocabulary

As you complete the Reading Notes, use these terms in your answers.

topography	Nile River	Kush	Canaan
vegetation	Egypt	Mediterranean Sea	Jordan River

Use the landscape drawing below to complete the following:

1. How did water affect people's choices of where to settle? Write three statements that answer this question.

   -
   -
   -

2. How did topography affect people's choices of where to settle? Write three statements that answer this question.

   -
   -
   -

3. How did vegetation affect people's choices of where to settle? Write three statements that answer this question.

   -
   -
   -

4. In the image below, circle (or draw) an example of each factor you described. Circle water related factors in *blue*, topography related factors in *orange*, and vegetation related factors in *green*.

© Teachers' Curriculum Institute

After reading Section 2 and examining the map in the section, follow the steps below.

1. Label these physical features on the map:

   - Mediterranean Sea
   - Red Sea
   - Nile River
   - Arabian Desert
   - Libyan Desert
   - Nubian Desert

Ancient Egypt and Kush

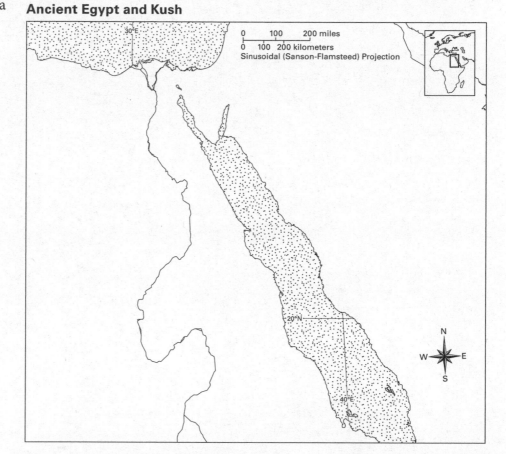

2. Draw the letter *H* or another simple symbol in all the places on the map where human settlements were located in this region.

3. Write a paragraph that answers this question: *How did geography affect people's choices of where to settle in ancient Egypt and Kush?* Use and underline at least five words or phrases from the Word Bank.

Word Bank
water
topography
vegetation
Mediterranean Sea
Red Sea
Nile River
Arabian Desert
Libyan Desert
Nubian Desert

After reading Section 3 and examining the map in the section, follow the steps below.

1. Label these physical features on the map:

   - Mediterranean Sea
   - Sea of Galilee
   - Dead Sea
   - Jordan River
   - Lebanon Mountains
   - Negev Desert
   - Syrian Desert

Ancient Canaan

2. Draw the letter *H* or another simple symbol in all the places on the map where human settlements were located in this region.

3. Write a paragraph that answers this question: *How did geography affect people's choices of where to settle in ancient Canaan?* Use and underline at least five words or phrases from the Word Bank.

Word Bank
water
topography
vegetation
Mediterranean Sea
Sea of Galilee
Dead Sea
Jordan River
Lebanon Mountains
Negev Desert
Syrian Desert
nomad

© Teachers' Curriculum Institute

PROCESSING

Draw a simple map of the state where you live. Your map should include the following:

- labels for three or more important physical features (bodies of water and landforms) in your state

- shading on the areas containing vegetation that is best suited for human settlement

- the letter *H* or another simple symbol to show the most likely locations of the first human settlements

Then write a short paragraph to answer this question: *How did geography affect early settlement in your state?* Your answer should include the names of at least two of the important physical features of your state and at least two of these terms: *water, topography, vegetation.*

The Ancient Egyptian Pharaohs

What did the pharaohs of ancient Egypt accomplish, and how did they do it?

PREVIEW

Carefully analyze the image and write your answers to the questions below.

1. What interesting details do you see in this postcard's image?

2. In whose honor do you think this monument was built?

3. Why do you think this monument was built to honor these four men?

4. What other monuments do you know that have been built to honor a person or group of people? Where are these monuments? Whom do they honor?

READING NOTES

Social Studies Vocabulary

As you complete the Reading Notes, use these terms in your answers.

pharaoh   Hatshepsut   Ramses II   treaty

Section 1

1. Follow these steps to complete the timeline below:

   - Draw a bar to represent how long each kingdom lasted. Use *red* for the Old Kingdom, *green* for the Middle Kingdom, and *blue* for the New Kingdom.
   - Label each bar with the name of the kingdom (Old, Middle, or New), and also write another name that the period is known by (Example: Age of Pyramids).
   - Underneath each bar, list one or two things that the period is known for.

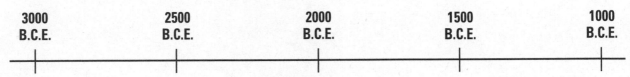

2. In the Venn diagram below, list at least one way that the pharaohs of ancient Egypt are similar to presidents in the United States today. Then list at least two ways that Egyptian pharaohs are different from U.S. presidents.

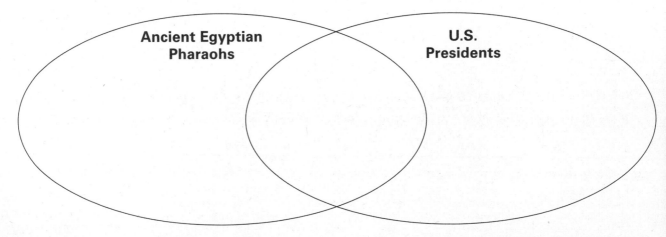

          © Teachers' Curriculum Institute

Section 2

Write a postcard to a friend or relative about the pharaoh Khufu and your visit to the Great Pyramid. Make sure your postcard includes the following:

- an appropriate greeting (such as "Dear Maria,") and closing (such as "See you soon!")

- information about the pharaoh Khufu, such as when he ruled, what kind of ruler he was, and what some of his important accomplishments were

- information about the Great Pyramid, such as how big it was, what it was made of, how long it took to build, and how the Egyptians might have built it

Sketch a stamp for the postcard by drawing a visual or symbol that relates to what you learned.

Dear _____,

The monument I just visited is _____

_____

_____

_____

It was built by the pharoah _____

_____

_____

_____

_____

Section 3

Write a postcard to a friend or relative about the pharaoh Senusret I and your visit to the White Chapel. Make sure your postcard includes the following:

- an appropriate greeting and closing
- information about the pharaoh Senusret I, such as when he ruled, what kind of ruler he was, and what some of his greatest accomplishments were
- information about the White Chapel, such as what it was made of, what kind of artwork it included, and how it was discovered by archaeologists

Sketch a stamp for the postcard by drawing a visual or symbol that relates to what you learned.

Dear _____,

Today, I learned about the pharaoh Senusret I _____

_____

_____

_____

I also saw the White Chapel. _____

_____

_____

_____

_____

© Teachers' Curriculum Institute

Section 4

Write a postcard to a friend or relative about the pharaoh Hatshepsut and your visit to the temple at Dayr al-Bahri. Make sure your postcard includes the following:

- an appropriate greeting and closing
- information about the pharaoh Hatshepsut, such as when she ruled, what was unique about her rule, and what she accomplished in relation to trade with other countries
- information about the temple at Dayr al-Bahri, such as where it was built and how were the outside and the inside walls decorated

Sketch a stamp for the postcard by drawing a visual or symbol that relates to what you learned.

Hello from Dayr al-Bahri !

Dear _____,

Today, I learned about the pharaoh Hatshepsut. _____

_____

_____

_____

I also visited her temple at Dayr al-Bahri. _____

_____

_____

_____

_____

Section 5

Write a postcard to a friend or relative about the pharaoh Ramses II (Ramses the Great) and your visit to the temple at Abu Simbel. Make sure your postcard includes the following:

- an appropriate greeting and closing
- information about the pharaoh Ramses II, such as when he ruled and why he was called Ramses the Great
- information about the temple at Abu Simbel, such as what the sculptures at the main entrance were, what caused a unique event to happen twice a year, and how the temple was saved from near destruction

Amazing Abu Simbel

Sketch a stamp for the postcard by drawing a visual or symbol that relates to what you learned.

Dear _____,

Today, I learned about the pharaoh Ramses II. _____

_____

_____

I also visited his temple at Abu Simbel. _____

_____

_____

PROCESSING

On a separate sheet of paper, write a paragraph answering the Essential Question:

What did the pharaohs of ancient Egypt accomplish, and how did they do it?

Support your answer with specific examples of great accomplishments of at least three pharaohs.

 © Teachers' Curriculum Institute

Preparing to Write: Comparing and Contrasting Then and Now

The techniques that archaeologists use as they study artifacts have changed over time. In the chart below, describe the methods used by scientists in the early 1900s, in the time of Howard Carter. Then describe how modern scientists, such as those who took part in the Egyptian Mummy Project, conduct research today. Explain the effects of each period's techniques on the mummies being studied.

	Archaeologists in the Early 1900s	Archaeologists Today
Techniques		
Effects		

Writing a Compare and Contrast Paragraph

In the space below, write a paragraph that compares and contrasts the techniques used by archaeologists studying ancient Egyptian mummies in the early 1900s and today. Describe the effects of each period's techniques on the mummies. Use the information in the chart you completed on the preceding page to organize and write your paragraph.

Use this rubric to evaluate your essay. Make changes to your work if you need to.

Score	Description
3	The paragraph includes information that is very relevant to the topic, and compares and contrasts the two periods. There are no spelling or grammar errors.
2	The paragraph includes information that is somewhat relevant to the topic, and compares or contrasts the two periods. There are some spelling or grammar errors.
1	The paragraph includes information that is not relevant to the topic and does not compare or contrast the two periods. There are many spelling or grammar errors.

© Teachers' Curriculum Institute

Daily Life in Ancient Egypt

How did social class affect daily life in ancient Egypt?

Using the list below, copy the name of each individual or group below onto the level of the pyramid where you think it belongs. For each name, write a short sentence to explain why you placed it at that level on the pyramid.

| Students | Principal | Teachers | Student Council | Office Staff | Assistant Principal |

My School's Social Pyramid

READING NOTES

Social Studies Vocabulary

As you complete the Reading Notes, use these terms in your answers.

social pyramid	status	peasant	hieroglyph
social class	noble	afterlife	

Section 1

1. Label the social class in ancient Egypt that belongs on each level of the social pyramid below. Draw a symbol or visual to represent each social class. Write a brief caption explaining what each symbol or visual means. An example is completed for you.

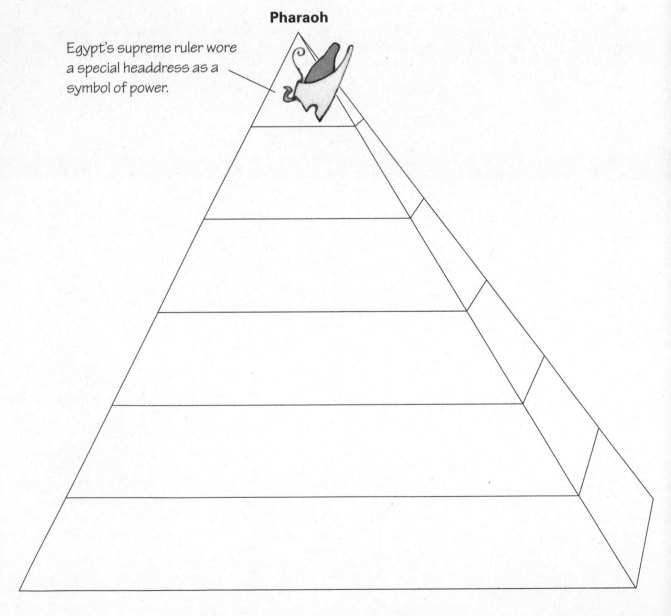

Pharaoh

Egypt's supreme ruler wore a special headdress as a symbol of power.

© Teachers' Curriculum Institute

2. Why was ancient Egyptian society structured like a pyramid?

3. How did religion affect the organization of the social pyramid?

4. In what ways did Egyptian women enjoy more freedom and rights than most women in the ancient world?

5. Why do you think that the social pyramid in ancient Egypt was rigid?

Section 2

1. On the social pyramid, outline and label the level that represents government officials.

2. Write down three or more important facts about the types of government officials and their responsibilities.

   •

   •

   •

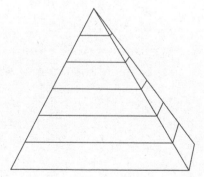

3. In complete sentences, answer this question: *How did the status of government official affect the daily lives of people in this social class?*

Section 3

1. On the social pyramid, outline and label the level that represents priests.

2. Write down three or more important facts about the types of priests and their duties.

   -
   -
   -

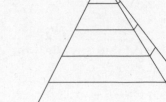

3. In complete sentences, answer this question: *How did the status of priest affect the daily lives of people in this social class?*

Section 4

1. On the social pyramid, outline and label the level that represents scribes.

2. Write down three or more important facts about scribe schools and the types of work scribes did.

   -
   -
   -

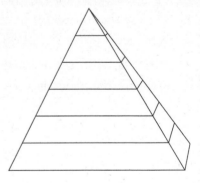

3. In complete sentences, answer this question: *How did the status of scribe affect the daily lives of people in this social class?*

© Teachers' Curriculum Institute

Section 5

1. On the social pyramid, outline and label the level that represents artisans.

2. Write down three or more important facts about the types of artisans and their work.

   -
   -
   -

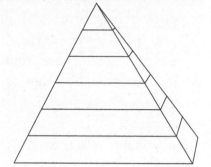

3. In complete sentences, answer this question: *How did the status of artisan affect the daily lives of people in this social class?*

Section 6

1. On the social pyramid, outline and label the level that represents peasants.

2. Write down three or more important facts about the work of peasants during the three seasons.

   -
   -
   -

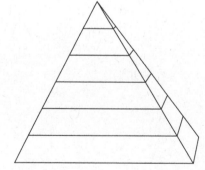

3. In complete sentences, answer this question: *How did the status of peasant affect the daily lives of people in this social class?*

PROCESSING

Compare at least three levels of the ancient Egyptian social pyramid to your school's social pyramid (from the Preview activity). For each level, identify the Egyptian and school group. Explain at least one way that the two groups are similar and at least one way that the two groups are different. A sample comparison for the top level on the pyramid is provided below.

The pharaoh in ancient Egypt is like my school principal because both have the most power and authority. The pharaoh in ancient Egypt differs from my school principal because the pharaoh was believed to be a god.

© Teachers' Curriculum Institute

INVESTIGATING PRIMARY SOURCES

Using Questions and Evaluating Sources

Think about what you know about scribes in ancient Egypt. What else do you want to learn about this group? List some questions you have about scribes.

Question 1:

Question 2:

Question 3:

Read Investigating Primary Sources, What Was It Like to Be a Scribe in Ancient Egypt?, in the Student Text. Use the primary sources in the reading and reliable sources from the Internet or books to answer the questions. For each source, consider if it helps answer the question and why it was created.

Answer 1:

Source:

Answer 2:

Source:

Answer 3:

Source:

Use the evidence you gathered to make a claim to this question: *What was it like to be a scribe in ancient Egypt?*

Claim:

Constructing an Argument

Create an argument to answer the question: *What was it like to be a scribe in ancient Egypt?* Your argument should:

- clearly state your claim.

- include evidence from multiple sources.

- provide explanations for how the sources support the claim.

Use this rubric to evaluate your argument. Make changes as needed.

Score	Description
3	The claim clearly answers the question. The argument uses evidence from two or more primary sources that strongly support the claim. The explanations accurately connect to the evidence and claim.
2	The claim answers the question. The argument uses evidence from one or more primary sources that support the claim. Some of the explanations connect to the evidence and claim.
1	The claim fails to answer the question. The argument lacks evidence from primary sources. Explanations are missing or are unrelated to the evidence and claim.

 © Teachers' Curriculum Institute

The Kingdom of Kush

How did location influence the history of Kush?

Follow these directions to create a sensory figure in the space below. A sensory figure is a simple drawing of a character and includes short descriptions of what that character sees, hears, touches, and feels.

- Draw a simple outline of a famous person. You can choose a historical figure or a present-day figure, such as a political leader, entertainer, athlete, actor, and so on. Title the drawing with the name of the person.

- Complete the statement in each box to describe four important things this person has seen, heard, touched, and felt (emotions) during his or her lifetime. Draw a line from each statement to the corresponding body part on the figure

With my eyes, I see...

With my ears, I hear...

With my heart, I feel...

With my hands, I touch...

READING NOTES

Social Studies Vocabulary

As you complete the Reading Notes, use these terms in your answers.

Meroë   dynasty   kandake

Section 1

Identify the location of Kush by completing the map below. Use one color to shade in Kush and the corresponding box in the key. Use a different color to shade in Egypt and the corresponding box in the key. Answer the questions to the right of the map.

Egypt and Kush, 1600–1100 B.C.E.

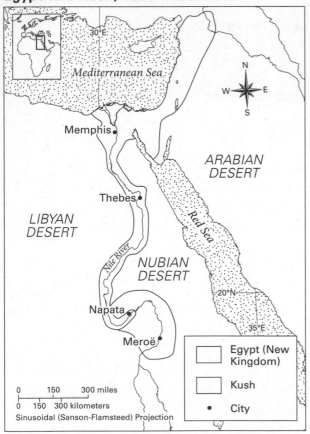

1. How did location and natural resources help Kush?

2. What did Kush trade with its neighbor, Egypt?

© Teachers' Curriculum Institute

For the sensory figure below, finish the statements to describe four important things a Kushite leader would have seen, heard, touched, and felt (emotions) during the historical period, 1600 to 1100 B.C.E. In your statements, include and underline all the words and phrases from the Word Bank. Use each word or phrase at least once. One example is done for you.

Word Bank	
gold	trading hub
Egypt	Egyptianized
tribute	independence

With my eyes, I see...

With my ears, I hear...

With my heart, I feel...

sad that my kingdom of Kush has become Egyptianized. We speak their language, worship their gods, and wear their style of clothing

With my hands, I touch...

In complete sentences, answer this question: *How did location influence Kush during this time period?*

Section 2

For the sensory figure below, finish the statements to describe four important things a Kushite leader would have seen, heard, touched, and felt (emotions) during the historical period, mid-700s to mid-600s B.C.E. In your statements, include and underline all the words and phrases from the Word Bank. Use each word or phrase at least once.

Word Bank	
armies	Kushite pharaohs
Egypt	Jebel Barkal
dynasty	Assyrians

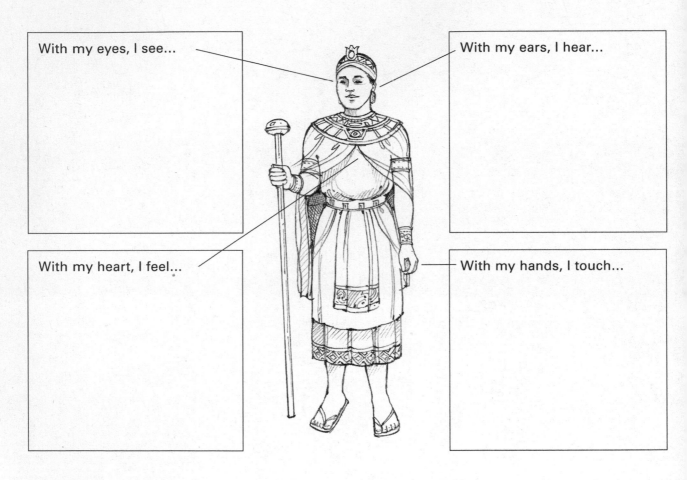

With my eyes, I see...

With my ears, I hear...

With my heart, I feel...

With my hands, I touch...

In complete sentences, answer this question: *How did location influence Kush during this time period?*

© Teachers' Curriculum Institute

Section 3

For the sensory figure below, finish the statements to describe
four important things a Kushite leader would have seen, heard,
touched, and felt (emotions) during the historical period
that began about 590 B.C.E. In your statements, include and
underline all the words and phrases from the Word Bank. Use
each word or phrase at least once.

Word Bank	
Meroë	resources
trade	weapons and tools
iron	

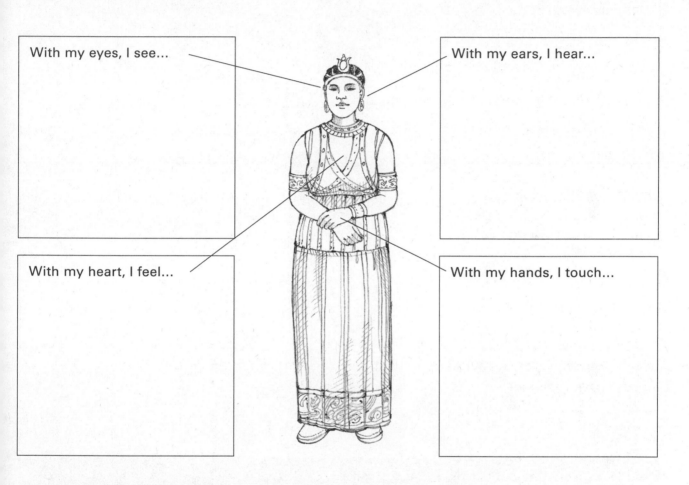

With my eyes, I see...

With my ears, I hear...

With my heart, I feel...

With my hands, I touch...

In complete sentences, answer this question: *How did location influence Kush
during this time period?*

© Teachers' Curriculum Institute

Section 4

For the sensory figure below, finish the statements to describe four important things a Kushite leader would have seen, heard, touched, and felt (emotions) during the period in which Kush split from Egypt. In your statements, include and underline all the words from the Word Bank. Use each word at least once.

Word Bank	
African	treaty
Meroitic	Roman
kandake	

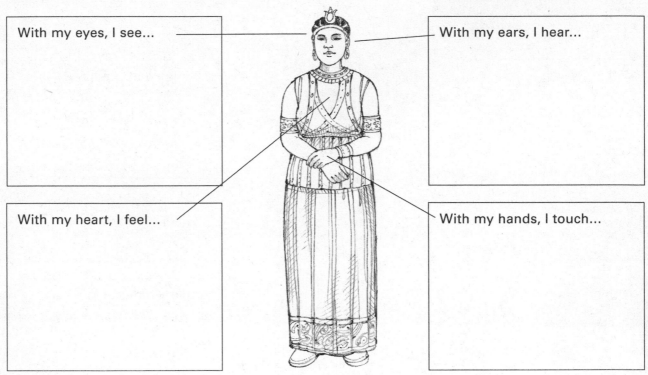

With my eyes, I see...

With my ears, I hear...

With my heart, I feel...

With my hands, I touch...

In complete sentences, answer this question: *How did location influence Kush during this time period?*

PROCESSING

On a separate sheet of paper, copy the timeline and dates below.

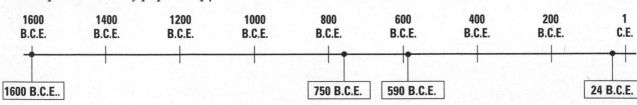

| 1600 B.C.E. | 1400 B.C.E. | 1200 B.C.E. | 1000 B.C.E. | 800 B.C.E. | 600 B.C.E. | 400 B.C.E. | 200 B.C.E. | 1 C.E. |

1600 B.C.E..   750 B.C.E.   590 B.C.E.   24 B.C.E.

Create an illustrated timeline of the history of Kush. For each date boxed on the timeline, identify the event, explain its importance, and draw a relevant symbol.

Below your timeline, respond in complete sentences to this question: *During which time period did location most influence Kush, and why?*

   © Teachers' Curriculum Institute

The Origins of Judaism

How did Judaism originate and develop?

Think of two historical figures who have been important in the development of the United States. List them below. Then write a sentence that explains each person's contributions to this country. Draw a symbol or visual to represent the contributions. An example is given for you.

Alice Paul

She led the fight for women to have the right to vote, which was finally achieved in 1920.

Figure 1:

Figure 2:

Social Studies Vocabulary

As you complete the Reading Notes, use these terms in your answers.

Torah	Judaism	Israel	Jerusalem	Exodus
Israelite	tradition	slavery	covenant	Ten Commandments

Section 1

Identify the sources that historians use to learn about the ancient Israelites. Which of these sources do you think is the most useful and why?

Complete the timeline below. For each of the boxed dates, write a brief caption describing the location and movement of the ancient Israelites around that time. Add a title for your timeline that summarizes its main idea.

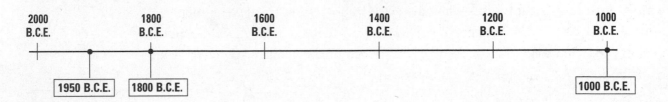

Section 2

For each Jewish leader on the matrix, describe one action he took as the leader of the ancient Israelites and one contribution that the Torah says he made to the development of Judaism.

Jewish Leader	Action as Leader	Contribution to Judaism
Abraham		
Moses		
David		
Solomon		

   © Teachers' Curriculum Institute

Abraham
אברהם

1. Describe one or more important actions taken by Abraham.

2. List at least two contributions that the Torah says Abraham made to the development of Judaism. For each one, explain why this contribution is significant.

   •

   •

3. Write a quotation from the Torah that shows one of these contributions.

4. Sketch a key artifact relating to Abraham. Write a caption explaining how this artifact relates to the life of Abraham, as described in the Torah.

Moses
מֹשֶׁה

1. Describe one or more important actions taken by Moses.

2. List at least two contributions that the Torah says Moses made to the development of Judaism. For each one, explain why this contribution is significant.

   •

   •

3. Write a quotation from the Torah that shows one of these contributions.

4. Sketch a key artifact relating to Moses. Write a caption explaining how this artifact relates to the life of Moses, as described in the Torah.

© Teachers' Curriculum Institute

David   Solomon
דוד   שלמה

1. Describe one or more important actions taken by David and by Solomon.

2. List at least two contributions that the Torah says David and Solomon made to the development of Judaism. For each contribution, explain why it is significant.

   -

   -

3. Write a quotation from the Hebrew Bible that shows one of these contributions.

4. Sketch a key artifact relating to David or Solomon. Write a caption explaining how this artifact relates to the life of David or Solomon, as described in the Torah.

PROCESSING

In the space below, first list one contribution that Abraham, Moses, David, and Solomon made to the origin and development of Judaism. Then, from your list, choose the individual who you think made the most significant contribution and explain your choice in a well-written paragraph.

© Teachers' Curriculum Institute

Learning About World Religions: Judaism

***What are the central teachings of Judaism, and why
did they survive to modern day?***

PREVIEW

Think of a tradition that is shared and preserved in your family. It might be
a favorite recipe, a story, an activity, or a special custom. Briefly describe your
tradition in the space below, and then answer the questions that follow.

My family tradition:

How long has your family had this tradition?

What challenges have you or your family faced in trying to preserve this tradition?

In what ways have you or your family tried to pass this tradition along to others?

READING NOTES

Social Studies Vocabulary

As you complete the Reading Notes, use these terms in your answers.

polytheism	Talmud	exile	Yavneh
monotheism	ethics	Jewish Diaspora	

Complete the matrix below by doing the following:

- In the first column, identify the four central beliefs and teachings of Judaism, as discussed in Section 1.
- In the second column, briefly describe each belief or teaching.
- In the third column, explain how each belief or teaching is influential today.

Four Central Teachings of Judaism	Description	Influence Today

© Teachers' Curriculum Institute

Section 2

A fellow student has questions about the beginning of the Jewish Diaspora. Create
a dialogue with the student. Fill in responses with sentences that answer the
student's questions.

Student:

*How did the Jewish Diaspora begin,
and why was it difficult for followers
of Judaism?*

You:

The Jewish Diaspora began in 597 B.C.E., when . . .

Student:

*Which foreign powers ruled Judah, and
how did they treat the Jews?*

You:

*The Babylonians were conquered in 539 B.C.E.
by the . . .*

Student:

*What happened after the Jews rose
up against the Romans in 66 C.E.? in
135 C.E.?*

You:

*The Jews kept the Romans out of Jerusalem for
three years, but in 70 C.E. . . .*

Learning About World Religions: Judaism **89**

Section 3

A fellow student has questions about how Judaism survived and developed during the Jewish Diaspora. Create a dialogue with the student. Fill in responses with sentences that answer the student's questions.

Student:

Where did the Jews live during the Jewish Diaspora?

You:

After losing control of their homeland, Jews were exiled . . .

Student:

Who was Yohanan ben Zakkai, and why was he significant?

You:

Yohanan ben Zakkai was a rabbi who . . .

Student:

What new practices developed over time that helped Judaism survive?

You:

New practices were introduced to ensure that . . .

© Teachers' Curriculum Institute

PROCESSING

Find a newspaper or magazine article about a current topic that reflects one of the four central teachings of Judaism. Then, write a paragraph in the space below that tells which teaching the article reflects and how.

Timeline Skills

Analyze the Unit 2 timeline in the Student Text. Also think about what you have learned in this unit. Then answer the following questions.

1. Which of these events happened first: Abraham's migration to Canaan, Kushite pharaohs rule Egypt, or the reign of Hatshepsut?

2. Who was responsible for building the Great Pyramid of Egypt?

3. About how many years after the reign of Khufu did Ramses the Great rule Egypt?

4. For about how long did the African kingdom of Kush exist?

5. About when did Hatshepsut rule Egypt, and what was significant about her reign as pharaoh?

6. Did the Kushite pharaohs rule Egypt before or after Ramses the Great?

7. During whose reign was the First Temple of Jerusalem built?

8. How many years were the Jews held in captivity in Babylon?

9. When did Kush attack Roman forts? What happened as a result?

10. What is significant about the event that took place in 135 C.E.?

© Teachers' Curriculum Institute

Critical Thinking

Use the timeline and the lessons in the unit to answer the following questions.

11. Both Egypt and Kush flourished along the Nile River during this time period. What geographic conditions supported the rise of civilization in this region?

12. How did the relationship between Egypt and Kush change over time?

13. According to the timeline, Abraham moved to Canaan in 1950 B.C.E.

    a. Why is this event significant in the development of Judaism?

    b. What other important contribution did Abraham make?

14. If you could add three more events to this timeline, which ones would you choose? List each event and explain why you think it is important enough to add to the timeline.

    a.

    b.

    c.

© Teachers' Curriculum Institute

UNIT **3**

Ancient India

Geography Challenge

Lesson 13: Geography and the Early Settlement of India

How did geography affect early settlement in India?

Lesson 14: Unlocking the Secrets of Mohenjodaro

What can artifacts tell us about daily life in Mohenjodaro?

Lesson 15: Learning About World Religions: Hinduism

What are the origins and beliefs of Hinduism?

Lesson 16: Learning About World Religions: Buddhism

What are the main beliefs and teachings of Buddhism?

Lesson 17: The First Unification of India

How did Ashoka unify the Mauryan Empire and spread Buddhist values?

Lesson 18: The Achievements of the Gupta Empire

Why is the period during the Gupta Empire known as a "golden age"?

Timeline Challenge

Ancient India

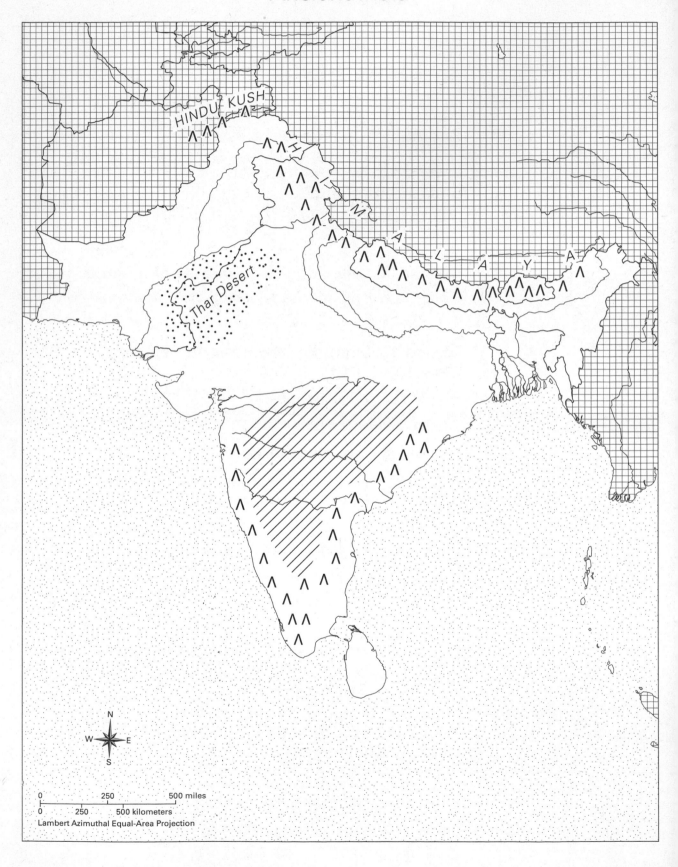

HINDU KUSH

H I M A L A Y A

Thar Desert

N
W E
S

0   250   500 miles
0   250   500 kilometers
Lambert Azimuthal Equal-Area Projection

© Teachers' Curriculum Institute

Geography Skills

Analyze the maps in "Setting the Stage" for Unit 3 in the Student Text. Then answer the following questions and fill out the map as directed.

1. Which bodies of water surround the southern part of ancient India? Label them on your map.

2. India is part of which continent?

3. Locate the Indus, Ganges, and Brahmaputra rivers on your map and label them.

4. Between what two mountain ranges is the Deccan Plateau located? Label these mountains and the plateau.

5. Locate the Himalayas on your map and circle the label. What makes this mountain range unique?

6. Look at the large map of ancient India in the Unit 3 "Setting the Stage" in the Student Text. Also look at the small map that shows the Mauryan Empire, an empire in ancient India. Describe the geographical boundaries of the Mauryan Empire.

7. Now look in the Student Text at the small map of the Gupta Empire. Which empire was larger, the Mauryan or the Gupta?

8. Into what body of water does the Indus River empty? The Ganges River?

Critical Thinking

Answer the following questions in complete sentences.

9. What geographic factors do you think encouraged the growth of civilization in the Indus River valley?

10. Predict how the location of the Himalayas, as well as their height, affected the development of civilization in ancient India.

11. What advantages would there have been to settling along the Indus River near its mouth at the Arabian Sea, as opposed to farther inland? What disadvantages might there have been to this location?

© Teachers' Curriculum Institute

Geography and the Early Settlement of India

How did geography affect early settlement in India?

You are part of a group of people living in ancient times. Your group needs to move, and you have been chosen to find a new location for resettlement. You travel until you find the perfect spot. No one lives there, and it has everything your group needs. What a location! Now you have to convince the others that this is the right place for your group's new home.

In the space below, draw and label a picture of the place you have chosen. Show the types of features and characteristics that make this an ideal place to settle.

READING NOTES

Social Studies Vocabulary

As you complete the Reading Notes, use these terms in your answers.

subcontinent   monsoon   plateau

1. Read Sections 1 to 8. Each section describes a different physical feature in India. As you read about each physical feature, label the feature on the appropriate place on the map.

Physical Features of India

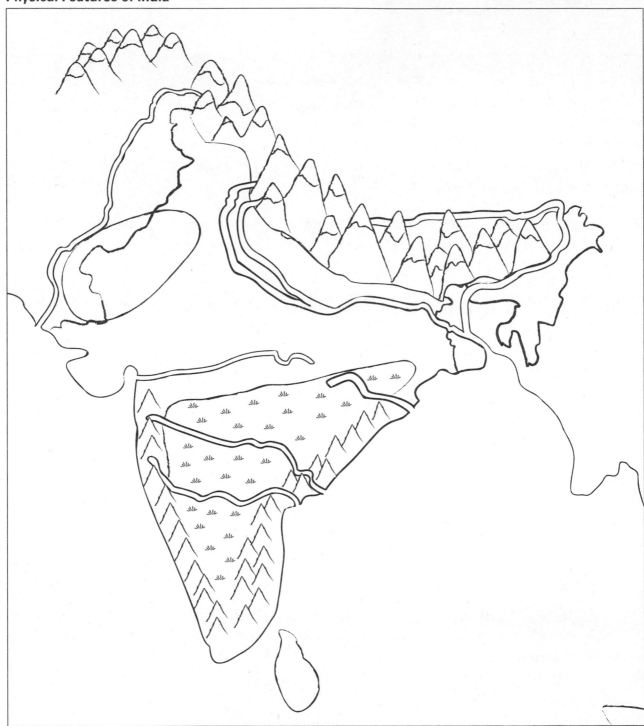

   © Teachers' Curriculum Institute

2. Work with your group to complete the table. Write a brief description of each physical feature. Then, in each box, rate the feature on a scale of 1 to 5. (1 = unsuitable for settlement, 5 = very suitable for settlement)

Physical Feature	Description	Rating
Brahmaputra River		
Deccan Plateau		
Eastern and Western Ghats		
Ganges River		
Himalaya Mountains		
Hindu Kush Mountains		
Indus River		
Thar Desert		

1. On the map, shade in the areas where early settlements in India were located. You may use the map in this section of the Student Text as a guide.

2. Why did the first people in India most likely choose to settle near rivers?

Early Settlements in India

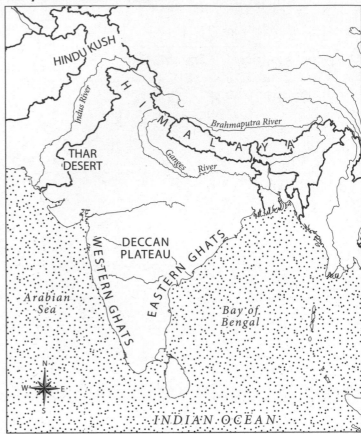

PROCESSING

Answer the following question in a well-written paragraph:

Why were the Indus and Ganges river valleys ideal locations for early settlement?

Support your answer by providing details on these two points:

• how the Indus and Ganges rivers affected the land nearby
• why two or more other physical features of India were unsuitable for settlement

© Teachers' Curriculum Institute

Preparing to Write: Finding Accurate Information

The article "Saving the Ganges" contains both facts and opinions. Facts are statements that can be proved or verified to be true. Opinions are statements of belief or judgment that cannot be proved and that differ among people.

List five *facts* the article tells you about the Ganges (not the *opinions* of the author or of the people mentioned in the article). For each fact, suggest some possible sources where the information might be found and verified.

Example: The Ganges begins where a number of small streams form from melting glaciers in the Himalaya Mountains. (maps, photographs)

1.

2.

3.

4.

5.

Planning a Research Report

Suppose that you wanted to write an environmental report on the water used by your community. Think about the article you have just read about the Ganges River. What important questions would you ask? What would be your sources of information? How could you evaluate the accuracy of the different sources?

Add three questions to the left column of the chart. In the right column, list source(s) that could most accurately help you find the answers. Two examples are provided.

What do you want to know?	What sources could you use for information?
How clean is the water in your community for drinking, cooking, and bathing?	Longtime residents of your community City water department City, county, or state health department Water-system engineers Web sites Maps
Where does our water supply come from?	City or town water department, maps

Use this rubric to evaluate your questions. Make changes to your work if you need to.

Score	Description
3	Each question is very relevant to the research topic. The source or sources will provide a reliable, factual answer to each question. There are no spelling or grammar errors.
2	The questions are somewhat relevant to the topic. Sources may be helpful in answering the question. There are some spelling or grammar errors.
1	Few or none of the questions are relevant to the topic. Sources are randomly chosen and may not reliably answer the questions. There are many spelling or grammar errors.

  © Teachers' Curriculum Institute

Unlocking the Secrets of Mohenjodaro

What can artifacts tell us about daily life in Mohenjodaro?

Examine this image of an ancient Indian artifact. Which of the three options below do you think is the accurate description of the object? Circle your choice and explain your answer.

I think this object is

- a table tennis paddle
- a mirror
- a serving plate

I think this because . . .

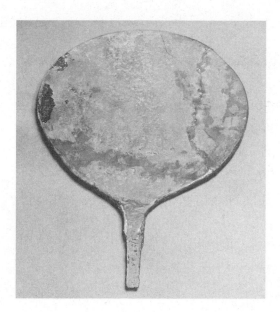

Social Studies Vocabulary

As you complete the Reading Notes, use these terms in your answers.

Mohenjodaro   Indus valley civilization
citadel   granary

1.   How do we know that Mohenjodaro was a carefully planned city?

2.   What do scientists believe happened to the Indus valley civilization?

Sections 2 to 9

If your class is doing the activity for this lesson, follow the instructions in your Reading Notes. *If your class is not doing the activity, use the images in the related sections of the Student Text to complete the drawings in the Reading Notes.*

Section 2: Station A

1.   Use the image of the artifact to complete the drawing.

2.   Record your ideas about what these objects may have been used for.

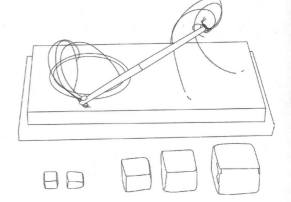

3.   Read Section 2. Record the archaeologists' ideas about these objects.

Section 3: Station B

1. Use the image of the artifact to complete the drawing.

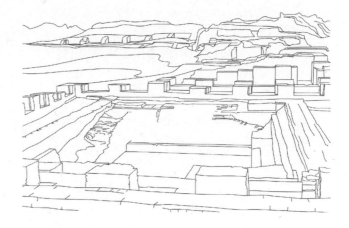

2. Record your ideas about what this structure may have been used for.

3. Read Section 3. Record the archaeologists' ideas about this structure.

Section 4: Station C

1. Use the images of the artifacts to complete the drawings.

2. Record your ideas about what these objects may have been used for.

3. Read Section 4. Record the archaeologists' ideas about these objects.

Section 5: Station D

1. Use the image of the artifact to complete the drawing.

2. Record your ideas about what this object may have been used for.

3. Read Section 5. Record the archaeologists' ideas about this object.

Section 6: Station E

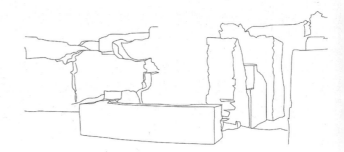

1. Use the image of the artifact to complete the drawing.

2. Record your ideas about what this structure may have been used for.

3. Read Section 6. Record the archaeologists' ideas about this structure.

   © Teachers' Curriculum Institute

Section 7: Station F

1. Use the image of the artifact to complete the drawing.

2. Record your ideas about what these structures may have been used for.

3. Read Section 7. Record the archaeologists' ideas about these structures.

Section 8: Station G

1. Use the image of the artifact to complete the drawing.

2. Record your ideas about what these objects may have been used for.

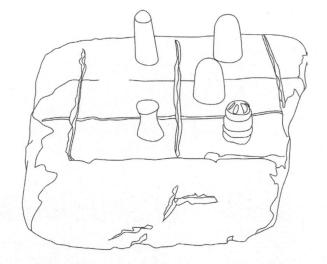

3. Read Section 8. Record the archaeologists' ideas about these objects.

Section 9: Station H

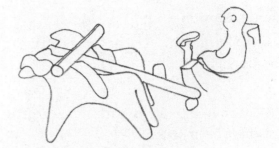

1. Use the image of the artifact to complete the drawing.

2. Record your ideas about what this object may have been used for.

3. Read Section 9. Record the archaeologists' ideas about this object.

PROCESSING

On a separate piece of paper, create a cover for an issue of *Dig It!* magazine, highlighting the archaeological discoveries made at Mohenjodaro. Your cover must include these elements:

- the title of the magazine (*Dig It!*) and an imaginative subtitle
- attractive visuals of three artifacts
- brief captions that explain what each artifact reveals about daily life in Mohenjodaro
- any other colorful and creative touches that make the cover more realistic

© Teachers' Curriculum Institute

Learning About World Religions: Hinduism

What are the origins and beliefs of Hinduism?

PREVIEW

Think about how religion affects life in the United States today. In the box below draw a picture that represents one way that religion influences the way of life of Americans in the 21st century.

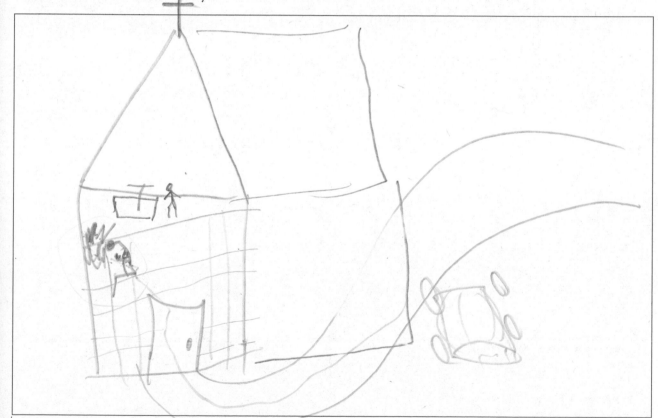

Write a sentence explaining what you drew.

Social Studies Vocabulary

As you complete the Reading Notes, use these terms in your answers.

Hinduism   monism

Vedas   dharma

Sanskrit   karma

varnas   reincarnation

jati   pilgrimage

caste

Section 1

1. Who founded the religion of Hinduism?

    No

2. What are the Vedas?

3. How have the Vedas influenced Hinduism?

Section 2

1. Use the spoke diagram below to identify and describe each of the four social classes, or varnas, described in the Vedas.

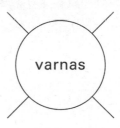

2. What was the role of jatis in Indian society?

3. In what ways did the caste system affect life in ancient India?

© Teachers' Curriculum Institute

Section 3

1. Record three key points that describe some Hindus' beliefs about Brahman.

    •

    •

    •

2. What are some ways these beliefs have affected life in India?

3. In the circle, draw a simple visual or symbol that illustrates these beliefs about Brahman.

Section 4

1. Record three key points that describe Hindu beliefs about deities.

   •

   •

   •

2. What are some ways these beliefs have affected life in India?

3. In the circle, draw a simple visual or symbol that illustrates these beliefs about deities.

Section 5

1. Record three key points that describe Hindu beliefs about dharma.

   •

   •

   •

2. What are some ways these beliefs have affected life in India?

3. In the circle, draw a simple visual or symbol that illustrates these beliefs about dharma.

© Teachers' Curriculum Institute

Section 6	Section 7

Section 6

1. Record three key points that describe Hindu beliefs about karma.

   •

   •

   •

2. What are some ways these beliefs have affected life in India?

3. In the circle, draw a simple visual or symbol that illustrates these beliefs about karma.

Section 7

1. Record three key points that describe Hindu beliefs about samsara.

   •

   •

   •

2. What are some ways these beliefs have affected life in India?

3. In the circle, draw a simple visual or symbol that illustrates these beliefs about samsara.

PROCESSING

Compose an acrostic poem for the word *Hinduism*. Follow these guidelines as you compose your poem, using the letters and space below.

- Include a sentence for each letter in the word *Hinduism*. A sample sentence is provided below.
- Use all of the Social Studies Vocabulary at least once and underline them in your completed poem.
- Summarize three ways Hindu beliefs have influenced life in India.

H indus are expected to follow a common <u>dharma</u>, or set of values, such as sharing food with others and practicing nonviolence.

I

N

D

U

I

S

M

© Teachers' Curriculum Institute

Learning About World Religions: Buddhism

What are the main beliefs and teachings of Buddhism?

What is happiness? How do you achieve happiness?

Answer these questions by filling in the thought bubble below with words and simple illustrations.

READING NOTES

Social Studies Vocabulary

As you complete the Reading Notes, use these terms in your answers.

Buddha	alms	Four Noble Truths
ascetic	nirvana	Eightfold Path
enlightenment	Buddhism	

Sections 1 to 5

Follow these steps to complete the Reading Notes for Sections 1–5. You may refer to the images in the Student Text as you work on each section.

Step 1: Above the image, create a short headline that captures why the scene is important. For example, a headline for Section 1 might be, "A Prince Is Born!"

Step 2: On or around the image, label three or more key details in the scene.

Step 3: Below the image, write a two- to three-sentence caption that describes what is happening in the scene.

Section 1

Headline: _____

Caption:

© Teachers' Curriculum Institute

Section 2

Headline: _____

Caption:

Section 3

Headline: _____

Caption:

Section 4

Headline: _____

Caption:

Section 5

Headline: _____

Caption:

© Teachers' Curriculum Institute

Section 6

1. Draw a simple illustration that represents the idea behind the Four Noble Truths. Write a brief caption to explain what the drawing shows.

2. Draw a simple illustration that represents the way that the Buddha thought people should take in order to end suffering. Write a brief caption to explain what the drawing shows.

3. Which of the Buddha's teachings do you find the most interesting, and why?

In the space below, write a paragraph that answers the Essential Question:

What are the main beliefs and teachings of Buddhism?

Be sure to include each Social Studies Vocabulary word at least once in your paragraph.

© Teachers' Curriculum Institute

INVESTIGATING PRIMARY SOURCES

Identifying Evidence

Consider this question: *What are different ways Buddhist principles were passed down?*

Examine the four primary sources in the reading, and write down evidence from each source that helps answer this question.

Primary Source 1	Primary Source 2
Primary Source 3	**Primary Source 4**

Use the evidence you gathered to make a claim to the question.

Claim:

Constructing an Argument

Create an argument to answer the question: *What are different ways Buddhist principles were passed down?* Your argument should:

- clearly state your claim.
- include evidence from multiple sources.
- provide explanations for how the sources support the claim.

Use this rubric to evaluate your argument. Make changes as needed.

Score	Description
3	The claim clearly answers the question. The argument uses evidence from two or more primary sources that strongly support the claim. The explanations accurately connect to the evidence and claim.
2	The claim answers the question. The argument uses evidence from one or more primary sources that support the claim. Some of the explanations connect to the evidence and claim.
1	The claim fails to answer the question. The argument lacks evidence from primary sources. Explanations are missing or are unrelated to the evidence and claim.

© Teachers' Curriculum Institute

The First Unification of India

How did Ashoka unify the Mauryan Empire and spread Buddhist values?

PREVIEW

1. Examine this drawing of a billboard. Underline or highlight the important words and phrases. Circle and label the visuals. Then answer the questions below.

2. What organization is being represented by the billboard? How do you know?

3. What is the main message of the billboard? What behavior does it encourage?

4. In what ways is this billboard effective in communicating its message? Do you think that it will make people change their behavior?

5. Where do we commonly find billboards? Why would the government and others place billboards there?

READING NOTES

Social Studies Vocabulary

As you complete the Reading Notes, use these terms in your answers.

Mauryan Empire   Ashoka   edict

Section 1

1. Shade in the Mauryan Empire and label its capital on the map.

2. Write a paragraph summarizing how Chandragupta Maurya built and ruled the Mauryan Empire. Use and underline these words or phrases in your summary: *kingdoms, conquer, unite, force, central government.*

Mauryan Empire

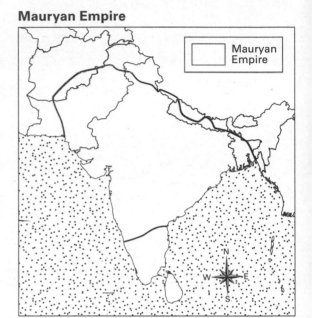

Section 2

Write a paragraph summarizing how Ashoka expanded and ruled the Mauryan Empire. Use and underline these words in your summary: *wars, reject, Buddhist, spread, practical.*

© Teachers' Curriculum Institute

1. Describe the four main goals of Ashoka's edicts on the pillars below.

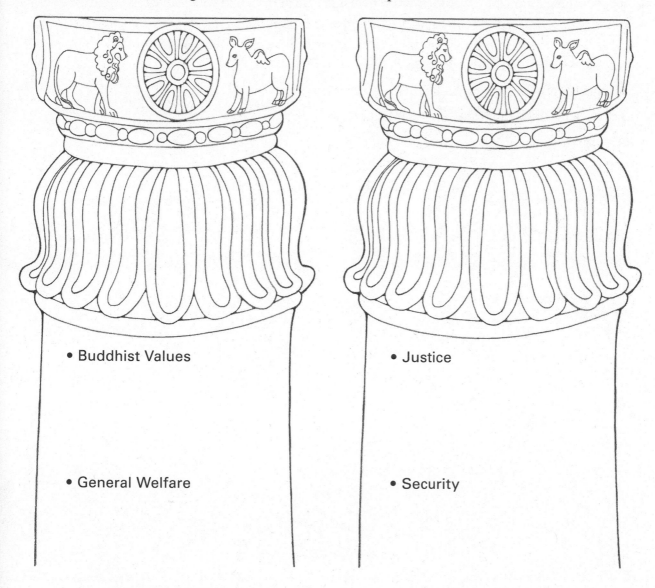

    • Buddhist Values   • Justice

    • General Welfare   • Security

2. How did these edicts help unify India?

3. How did Ashoka help spread Buddhism?

PROCESSING

Today's leaders communicate information by using a variety of methods. These include newspapers, radio, television, and the Internet. Suppose that Ashoka was also able to use the Internet to post his edicts and share his goals. Write a blog post for Ashoka's Web site. Follow these guidelines:

- Include a Web site address and name.
- Explain who Ashoka is and why he is important.
- Identify his four main goals.
- Include an excerpt from one of his edicts.
- Use clever and creative touches to make the blog more realistic.

© Teachers' Curriculum Institute

The Achievements of the Gupta Empire

Why is the period during the Gupta Empire known as a "golden age"?

Historians sometimes use the term "golden age" to describe a specific time period in history. Consider this term by answering the following questions. You may write or draw your responses.

What do you think a "golden age" is?

What might a "golden age" look like in an ancient civilization? Think about each of the following areas and describe it in a "golden age.":

Government	
Arts	
Writing	
Technology	
Education	

READING NOTES

Social Studies Vocabulary

As you complete the Reading Notes, use these terms in your answers.

Gupta Empire   province   philosophy

alliance   golden age

Section 1

1. How did the Guptas build and expand their empire?

2. Compare and contrast the governments of the Mauryan Empire and the Gupta Empire by completing the Venn diagram below. List the similarities between the empires in the overlapping area of the diagram. List the differences between the empires on the appropriate sides of the diagram.

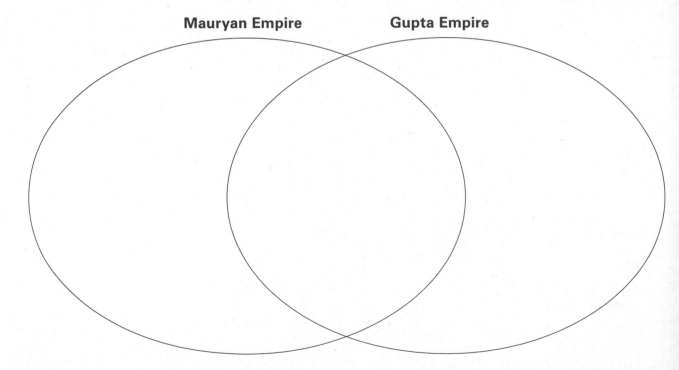

Mauryan Empire   **Gupta Empire**

          © Teachers' Curriculum Institute

3. Shade in the Gupta Empire on the map. Fill in the box in the key to match the color of the area you shade on the map.

Achievements of the Gupta Empire, 320–550 C.E.

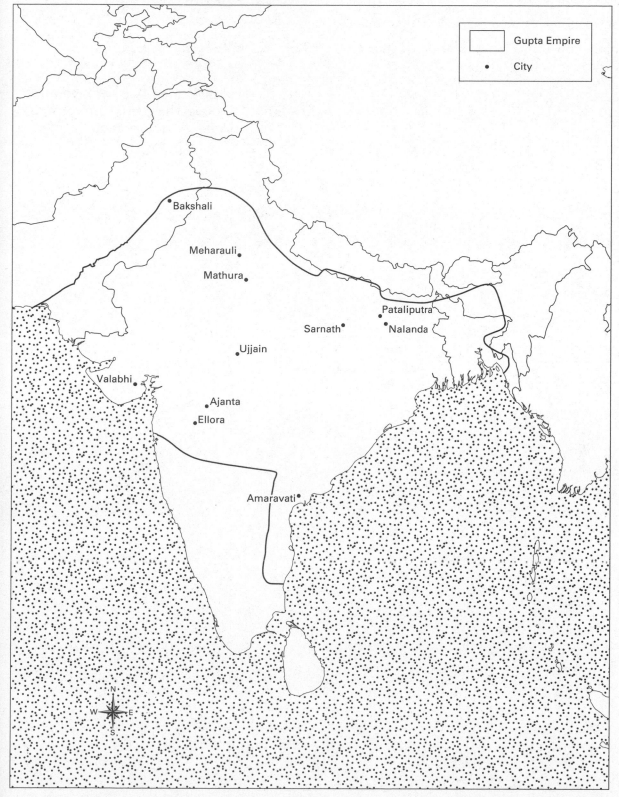

© Teachers' Curriculum Institute

As you read each section, complete the matrix for that section.

- List the achievement and draw a simple symbol that represents the achievement.
- Describe three or more important details about the achievement.
- Explain how this achievement shows that the Gupta Empire was a "golden age."

Section	Achievement and Symbol	Details About the Achievement	How does this achievement show that the Gupta Empire was a "golden age"?
2			
3			
4			

© Teachers' Curriculum Institute

Section	Achievement and Symbol	Details About the Achievement	How does this achievement show that the Gupta Empire was a "golden age"?
5			
6			
7			
8			

PROCESSING

Write a paragraph that answers the Essential Question: *Why is the period during the Gupta Empire known as a "golden age"?*

In your paragraph, introduce the Gupta Empire and define in your own words the term "golden age." To support your answer, use at least three examples of achievements you learned about on your tour of ancient India.

© Teachers' Curriculum Institute

Timeline Skills

Analyze the Unit 3 timeline in the Student Text. Also think about what you have learned in this unit. Then answer the following questions.

1. According to the timeline, about when did people first settle India? Where did they settle?

2. About how many years after the decline of the Harappan civilization was India first united?

3. Use the timeline to identify one characteristic of the Harappan civilization.

4. What is the connection between the Vedas and the development of Hinduism?

5. How old was Siddhartha when he became the Buddha and established Buddhism?

6. Which empire united India first—Gupta or Mauryan?

7. About when did India's golden age begin, and during which empire?

8. About how many years existed between the Mauryan and the Gupta empires? What was India like during this time?

9. Why would it have been impossible for Ashoka to spread Buddhist values before about 528 B.C.E.?

10. How does the timeline help explain why the *Aryabhatiya* was published in about 499 C.E.?

Critical Thinking

Use the timeline and the lessons in the unit to answer the following questions.

11. Why did it take about 35 years for Siddhartha to become the Buddha? Support your answer by describing at least two examples from Siddhartha's life.

12. The Mauryan Empire reached its height during the reign of King Ashoka. What are two of Ashoka's actions that might explain why?

13. India's golden age occurred during the Gupta Empire.

    a. How did the Guptas' ruling strategy help promote a golden age?

    b. Describe one significant achievement that happened during this period.

14. If you could add two more events to this timeline, which ones would you choose? List each event and explain why you think it is important enough to add to the timeline.

    a.

    b.

© Teachers' Curriculum Institute

Ancient China

Geography Challenge

Lesson 19: Geography and the Early Settlement of China
How did geography affect life in ancient China?

Lesson 20: The Shang Dynasty
What do Shang artifacts reveal about this civilization?

Lesson 21: Three Chinese Philosophies
How did Confucianism, Daoism, and Legalism influence political rule in ancient China?

Lesson 22: The First Emperor of China
Was the Emperor of Qin an effective leader?

Lesson 23: The Han Dynasty
In what ways did the Han dynasty improve government and daily life in China?

Lesson 24: The Silk Road
How did the Silk Road promote an exchange of goods and ideas?

Timeline Challenge

Ancient China

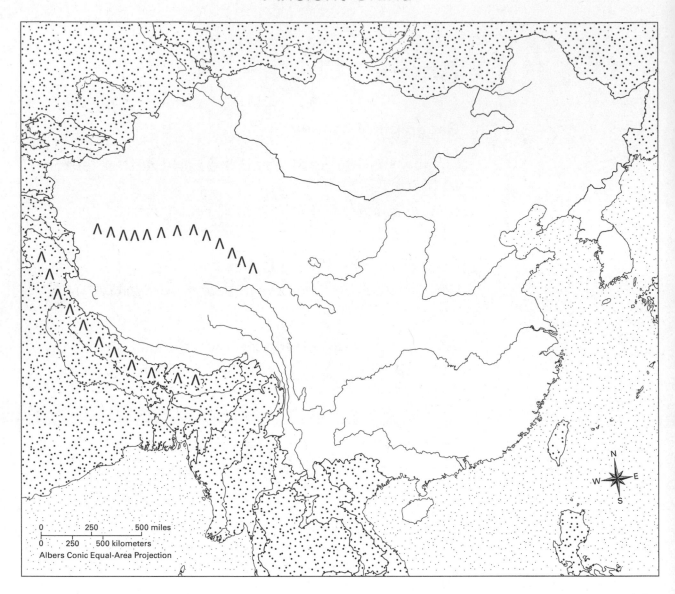

© Teachers' Curriculum Institute

Geography Skills

Analyze the maps in "Setting the Stage" for Unit 4 in the Student Text. Then answer the following questions and fill out the map as directed.

1. Locate the Huang He (Yellow River) and the Chang Jiang (Yangtze River) on your map. Label them.

2. The Plateau of Tibet is located between what two mountain ranges? Label the mountain ranges and the plateau on your map.

3. Locate the Taklimakan and the Gobi deserts on your map. Label them.

4. Locate the Yellow Sea, the East China Sea, and the South China Sea on your map. Label them.

5. In what ways might these seas have influenced China's history?

6. Use the maps in the Student Text to compare the sizes of the Shang, Zhou, Qin, and Han empires. Which empire controlled the largest area?

7. Under which empire did ancient China control territories that are not part of present-day China?

8. What geographical features are shared by all four ancient Chinese empires?

Critical Thinking

Answer the following questions in complete sentences.

9. The majority ethnic group in China today calls itself the "Han people." Why do you think this is so?

10. If you could choose anywhere in ancient China to build a new city, in which location do you think your city would have the greatest chance of success? Why?

11. Why do you think that the area controlled by earlier dynasties grew larger under the control of each new dynasty?

© Teachers' Curriculum Institute

Geography and the Early Settlement of China

How did geography affect life in ancient China?

Physical Features

1. Circle the physical features that are found in your community.

bay	creek	desert	hills
lake	mountains	ocean	plains
plateau	river	valley	coastal plain

2. How do physical features influence your community?

Climate

1. Circle the words that describe your community's climate.

Summer temperature:	hot	mild	cold
Winter temperature:	hot	mild	cold
Precipitation (rain and snow):	light	moderate	heavy

2. How does climate influence your community?

Vegetation

1. What natural vegetation do you have in your community? For example, does your community have grasslands, forests, scrub vegetation, or no vegetation?

2. How does the natural vegetation influence your community?

READING NOTES

Social Studies Vocabulary

As you complete the Reading Notes, use these terms in your answers.

region   oasis   loess
climate   North China Plain   tributary

Section 1

Why was Inner China more attractive than Outer China to early settlers? Include at least two specific physical features in your answer.

Sections 2 to 6

In each box below, write at least three adjectives or phrases that describe the geographic region discussed in that section of the Student Text. Consider each region's physical features, climate, and vegetation.

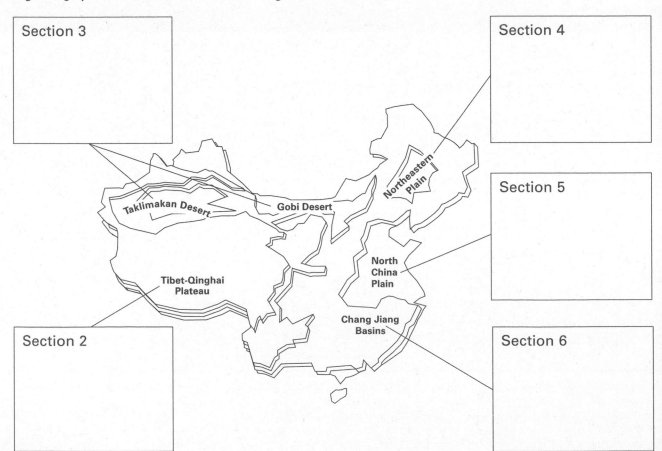

Section 3

Section 4

Section 5

Section 2

Section 6

Taklimakan Desert

Gobi Desert

Northeastern Plain

Tibet-Qinghai Plateau

North China Plain

Chang Jiang Basins

© Teachers' Curriculum Institute

If your class is doing the activity for this lesson, follow the instructions in your Reading Notes. *If your class is not doing the activity, use the information in the related sections of the Student Text to complete Part 1 of the Reading Notes for Sections 7 to 9.*

Section 7

Part 1:

Using only your geographic poster, give three reasons that support this hypothesis: *Most early people settled on the North China Plain because of its geography.* (**Hint:** Consider including reasons why other regions would not be good for settlement.)

Reasons that support this hypothesis:

1.

2.

3.

Part 2:

1. Read Section 7. How were the first people to live in China affected by geography?

2. On the map below, draw in and label the Huang He. Color the North China Plain the color of the soil found there.

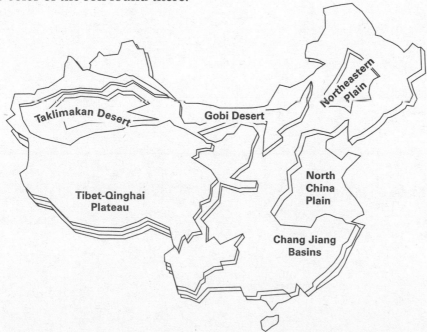

Part 1:

Using only your geographic poster, give three reasons that support this hypothesis: *China was isolated from other civilizations because of its geography.* (**Hint:** Consider how physical features and climate might affect travel, trade, and the spread of ideas.)

Reasons that support this hypothesis:

1.

2.

3.

Part 2:

1. Read Section 8. Add any additional information that shows why China was isolated from other civilizations because of its geography.

2. On the map, color the areas that caused China to be isolated from other civilizations.

    © Teachers' Curriculum Institute

Section 9

Part 1:

Using only your geographic poster, give three reasons that support this hypothesis: *Because of geography, several ways of life developed in China.* (**Hint:** Consider how geography might affect how people lived, what they ate, or what kinds of shelter they used.)

Reasons that support this hypothesis:

1.

2.

3.

Part 2:

1. Read Section 9. Add any additional information that shows why several ways of life developed in China because of geography.

2. In each box, draw one type of food, shelter, or economic activity (such as farming or herding animals) that might have been found in that region.

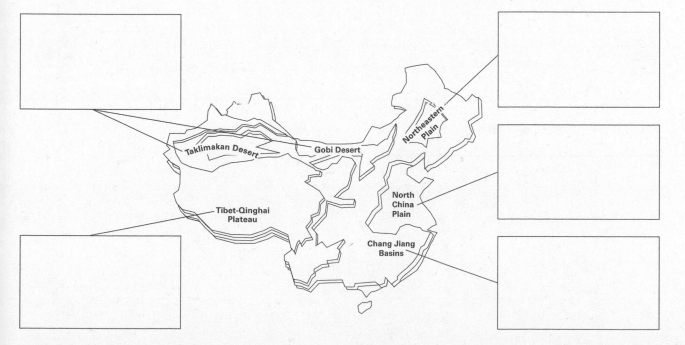

PROCESSING

The Chinese often drew pictures on scrolls to illustrate the landscape. Choose two of China's geographic regions. On the scroll below, use at least four colors to illustrate the geography and way of life in each region. Place your drawings of one region on the left side, and the other region on the right side. Show these elements:

- physical features, climate, and vegetation
- clothing, food, shelter, and economic activities of people living in that region

Write a paragraph that describes the ways in which the two regions are similar to and different from each other.

© Teachers' Curriculum Institute

The Shang Dynasty

2021

What do Shang artifacts reveal about this civilization?

979 years

PREVIEW

You are an archaeologist in the year 3000. You have recently unearthed several artifacts. Each relates to one characteristic of the civilization of the United States.

futuristic

3,000 AD

In the chart, name an artifact for each characteristic of American civilization. Then tell what you think the artifact reveals about the characteristic it relates to. For example, if you found a crown, you could write this statement: "This civilization might have been governed by a king or a queen."

Characteristic of the Civilization	Artifact	What This Artifact Reveals
Government *North Dakota*	*Mount Rushmore*	*6/7*
Social Structure *Florida Georgia*	*slave trade Blocks*	
Religion	*Nat'l Cathedral*	
Writing	*Jefferson's Bible*	
Art	*Sept. 11 20 memorial*	
Technology *Aviation Museum Pentagon Bldg*	*Silicon Valley major Headquarters Apple History museum*	

1750 - 1040 BCE

READING NOTES

Social Studies Vocabulary

As you complete the Reading Notes, use these terms in your answers.

Anyang   clan   ancestor worship

Shang dynasty   bronze   oracle bone

Section 1

1. Where were the ruins of a Shang city discovered?

    Anyang

2. Describe what archaeologists have discovered about Shang cities.

   - Bones unearthed - human sacrifice, animal → To go w/ King to
   - Artisan workshop   next world
   - Palace - w/ 9 royal Tomb   - Metal containing
                                 - weapons, jade, chariots

Section 2

For the sensory figure below, complete the statements to describe four important things a Shang warrior would have seen, heard, touched, and felt (emotions) as a member of the Shang army. In your statements, include and underline all the words from the Word Bank. Use each word at least once.

Word Bank

king

clan

bronze

chariot

With my ears, I hear . . .

With my eyes, I see . . .

With my heart, I feel . . .

With my hands, I touch . . .

© Teachers' Curriculum Institute

Complete the chart below by writing the name of the appropriate social class in each box. Then draw an artifact that an archaeologist might find relating to this social class and write a caption about it. The first box is completed as an example.

Social Classes in the Shang Dynasty

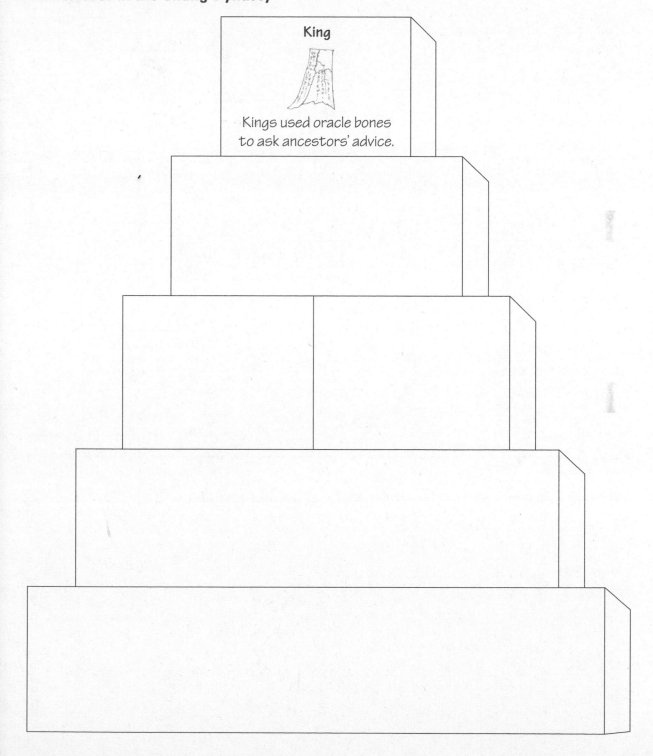

King

Kings used oracle bones to ask ancestors' advice.

For the sensory figure below, finish the statements to describe four important things a Shang king would have seen, heard, touched, and felt (emotions) about religion. In your statements, include and underline all the words from the Word Bank. Use each word at least once.

Word Bank

ancestor

offerings

duty

oracle bone

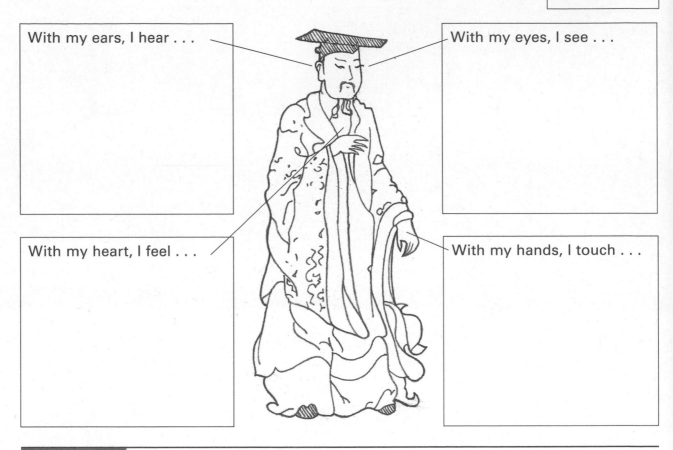

With my ears, I hear . . .

With my eyes, I see . . .

With my heart, I feel . . .

With my hands, I touch . . .

Section 5

1. On what objects were the first examples of Chinese writing found?

2. What is a logograph?

3. Why was a written language important in Chinese history?

© Teachers' Curriculum Institute

Section 6

1. Identify two materials used by Shang artists. For each material, list an example of an art piece that might be created using it.

2. Describe some ways that Shang artisans decorated vessels and other objects.

Section 7

1. Complete the spoke diagram below by naming the types of bronze tools of war made by Shang artisans. Put a star next to the item you think most helped strengthen the Shang army, and explain why you chose it.

Bronze Tools of War

2. Why were bronze-making skills important to the Shang dynasty?

In each box of the flowchart below, explain one reason why the Shang dynasty fell.

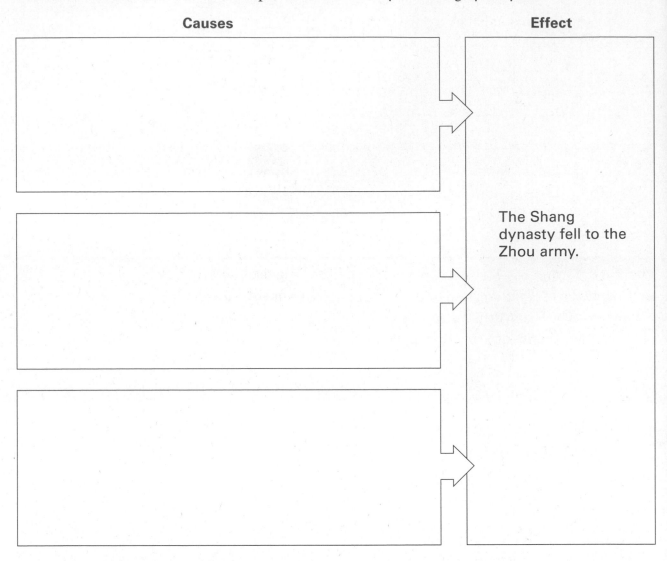

Causes

Effect

The Shang dynasty fell to the Zhou army.

PROCESSING

On a separate piece of paper, design a museum exhibit about the Shang dynasty. For your exhibit, select *one* of the characteristics of civilization (*government, social structure, religion, writing, art,* or *technology*), and include the following elements:

- a catchy exhibit title to draw visitors' attention
- a drawing of three artifacts that relate to the chosen characteristic
- a label to identify each of the three artifacts
- a plaque that summarizes what the three artifacts reveal about the characteristic in Shang society
- any other creative touches that make the exhibit more realistic

© Teachers' Curriculum Institute

Three Chinese Philosophies

How did Confucianism, Daoism, and Legalism influence political rule in ancient China?

PREVIEW

Which of the following approaches do you think would be most effective in dealing with school violence such as fighting and bullying? Write a paragraph at the bottom of this page that explains your answer.

Approach 1: Assign violent students a "big brother" or "big sister" who is a respected older student in another grade. The big brother or sister would teach the student how to behave properly.

Approach 2: Allow students guilty of fighting or bullying to go unpunished, hoping that they will eventually learn from their mistakes and correct their behavior.

Approach 3: Have school authorities publish the rules for unacceptable behavior and assign harsh punishments for violating those rules. For example, "students caught fighting will be expelled."

READING NOTES

Social Studies Vocabulary

As you complete the Reading Notes, use these terms in your answers.

Zhou dynasty   Confucianism   yin and yang

Mandate of Heaven   civil servant   Legalism

feudalism   Daoism

Section 1

1. Review this scenario: "A dynasty has ruled China for 100 years. This year, a severe drought is causing many to starve to death." From what you know of the Mandate of Heaven, why did the drought occur, and what action can be taken?

2. For each person below, write a speech bubble describing his or her role in the Zhou dynasty's feudal system. Then add an appropriate facial expression.

King   **Lord**   **Peasant**

3. Describe the Warring States period by filling in the warriors' banners below. In the banner to the left, explain what caused this period of instability. In the banner to the right, describe what happened as a result of this period.

Causes   **Results**

 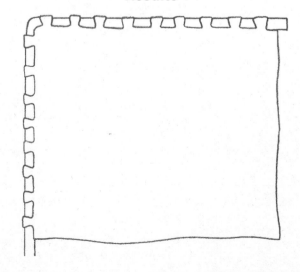

          © Teachers' Curriculum Institute

Section 2

In accordance with Confucian traditions, respect your teacher by answering the questions correctly.

1. Who was Confucius?

2. What was China like during his lifetime?

3. According to Confucius, what are the five basic relationships?

4. How should people act in these basic relationships?

5. What influence did Confucius have on Chinese government?

6. Write a caption below this image that would make your elders proud.

Section 3

In accordance with Daoist traditions, choose any technique that helps you demonstrate an understanding of the following questions about Daoism. You may write in complete sentences, use bullets, make drawings, or use another method that shows your understanding of this material.

1. Who was Laozi?

2. According to Daoism, how should people discover ways to behave?

3. What are yin and yang?

4. According to Daoists, how should rulers behave?

5. Perhaps you could write a caption below this image.

© Teachers' Curriculum Institute

Section 4

In accordance with Legalist traditions, follow the class rules as you answer the questions below. Do not make any errors. Memorize all answers.

1. Who was Hanfeizi?

2. According to Hanfeizi, what was the only way to create a strong society?

3. How did Hanfeizi believe a ruler should govern?

4. How did the members of the Qin dynasty apply the teachings of Hanfeizi?

5. Write a caption below this image, right now!

PROCESSING

Complete each of the following steps.

1. Describe your family's policy on homework. For example, do you have a special place to work? Can you listen to music, use the computer, or watch television while doing your homework? Does someone help you? Are there consequences for failing to do your homework?

2. Which of the following schools of thought is most like your family's policy toward homework: Confucianism, Daoism, or Legalism? Explain your answer.

3. Teach your parent or guardian about Confucianism, Daoism, and Legalism.

4. Ask your parent or guardian to decide whether the family's homework policy is most like the practices of Confucianism, Daoism, or Legalism. Write down his or her answer.

5. Discuss with your parent or guardian the answers to Question 2 and Question 4. Do your answers agree? If not, talk about why your answers differ. Then have your parent or guardian sign below.

Parent/Guardian Signature: _____

© Teachers' Curriculum Institute

The First Emperor of China

Was the Emperor of Qin an effective leader?

Place an *X* in the column that indicates whether you think each of the actions described below is evidence that a leader is effective or ineffective.

Leader	Effective	Ineffective
A leader who has absolute control over his people		
A leader who unifies the government		
A leader who makes laws for everyone to follow		
A leader who protects his people from invaders		
A leader who has his opponents killed		
A leader whose legacy lasts years beyond his death		

Which *one* of the actions makes a leader the *most effective*? Which *one* of the actions makes a leader the *least effective*? Explain your choices.

READING NOTES

Social Studies Vocabulary

As you complete the Reading Notes, use these terms in your answers.

Qin Shi Huangdi   Great Wall   immortal

standardize   censor

Section 1

Step 1: In the image at right, circle and label three interesting details. Then, in the space below, explain what you think these details reveal about the Emperor of Qin. You may also look at this image in Section 1 of the Student Text.

Step 2: Read Section 1. Answer the questions below in complete sentences.

1. Did Qin Shi Huangdi's control of China help or hurt the country? Explain.

2. How did Qin Shi Huangdi end feudalism? Why did he do this?

Step 3: Did the Emperor of Qin's efforts to control China make him an effective ruler? Mark your answer with an X on the spectrum below.

Very
Ineffective

Very
Effective

© Teachers' Curriculum Institute

Step 1: In the images at right, circle and label three interesting details. Then, in the space below, explain what you think these details reveal about the Emperor of Qin. You may also look at these images in Section 2 of the Student Text.

Step 2: Read Section 2. Answer the questions below in complete sentences.

1. Why did the Emperor of Qin create a unified set of laws? How did his Legalist beliefs affect these laws?

2. How did Qin Shi Huangdi improve trade and writing in China?

Step 3: Did the Emperor of Qin's efforts to standardize Chinese culture make him an effective ruler? Mark your answer with an *X* on the spectrum below.

Very
Ineffective

Very
Effective

© Teachers' Curriculum Institute

Step 1: In the image at right, circle and label three interesting details. Then, in the space below, explain what you think these details reveal about the Emperor of Qin. You may also look at this image in Section 3 of the Student Text.

Step 2: Read Section 3. Answer the questions below in complete sentences.

1. How did the emperor protect China's northern border?

2. Who constructed the Great Wall? What difficulties did they face?

Step 3: Did the Emperor of Qin's efforts to protect China's northern border make him an effective ruler? Mark your answer with an X on the spectrum below.

Very
Ineffective

Very
Effective

© Teachers' Curriculum Institute

Step 1: In the image at right, circle and label three interesting details. Then, in the space below, explain what you think these details reveal about the Emperor of Qin. You may also look at this image in Section 4 of the Student Text.

Step 2: Read Section 4. Answer the questions below in complete sentences.

1. Why was there a conflict between Confucian scholars and the emperor?

2. What did the emperor do to prevent people from learning about Confucianism?

Step 3: Did the Emperor of Qin's efforts to end opposition make him an effective ruler? Mark your answer with an *X* on the spectrum below.

Very
Ineffective

Very
Effective

1. Explain whether you think the Emperor of Qin achieved each of these goals:

   Goal 1: To become immortal

   Goal 2: To be remembered for a long time

2. List three things that were buried in the Emperor of Qin's tomb. What do these items reveal about the emperor?

PROCESSING

On a separate piece of paper, complete one of the two activities described here, depending on your answer to this question: *Do you think Qin Shi Huangdi was an effective or an ineffective ruler?* If you believe he was effective, design a commemorative plaque. If you believe he was ineffective, design a "wanted" poster. Your plaque or poster must contain the following:

• a title that indicates whether it is a commemorative plaque or a "wanted" poster

• a picture of the emperor

• at least three actions of the emperor that justify this plaque or poster, with illustrations for each action

   © Teachers' Curriculum Institute

Preparing to Write: Considering Great Monuments

Many people who travel to China feel that they must visit the Great Wall. Why do you think this is so?

What natural or human-made monument in your state or community is visited by tourists? What is special about it?

What are some similarities between your state's monument and China's Great Wall? What are some differences between them?

Monuments often attract commercial and recreational activities. What kinds of activities do you think should be allowed at such monuments? What activities do you think should not be allowed? Explain your reasoning.

Examples: Selling souvenirs; holding parties at the site; taking materials from the site for personal use or for use in home or road building

Writing a Diary Entry

Suppose that you are visiting the Great Wall of China. Write a diary entry about your visit. Describe in detail what you see there. Include facts about the wall, information the local people might tell you, and your own impressions. Use details from the article you have just read, and from the accompanying photographs, to help you write your entry. Add sketches or other visuals to add interest to your diary entry.

Use this rubric to evaluate your diary entry. Make changes to your work if you need to.

Score	Description
3	Each point is very relevant to the topic and is supported by the text and visuals. There are no spelling or grammar errors.
2	The points are somewhat relevant to the topic. Some statements may not be supported by the article or the visuals. There are some spelling or grammar errors.
1	Few or none of the points are relevant to the topic. Statements have little or no connection to the facts as given in the article or shown in the visuals. There are many spelling or grammar errors.

 © Teachers' Curriculum Institute

The Han Dynasty

In what ways did the Han dynasty improve government and daily life in China?

For each question below, review the image your teacher projects. Then circle the answer you guess is correct.

Warfare

1. In addition to scaring away enemies, how else did the kite help the Han army?

   A. It was used to send messages.

   B. It was used to deliver supplies.

   C. It provided light during night attacks.

Government

2. Who did the Han dynasty choose as government officials?

   A. those who wrote the best poems

   B. those who were already teachers

   C. those who scored well on exams

Agriculture

3. How did wheelbarrows help Han farmers?

   A. They made watering crops easier.

   B. They let farmers plant more land.

   C. They helped farmers move products.

Industry

4. How did the deep-digging drill increase the Hans' supply of salt?

   A. got salt water from deep in the ground

   B. dug pits to get salt from seawater

   C. made storage bins to keep salt dry

Art

5. Which of the following Han inventions helps artists and scholars?

   A. paper

   B. carpets

   C. paintbrushes

Medicine

6. Why would a Chinese doctor stick needles into a person's body?

   A. to release evil spirits

   B. to punish bad people

   C. to balance yin and yang

Science

7. What could the Han learn from the earthquake device they invented?

   A. the depth of an earthquake

   B. the direction of an earthquake

   C. the damage caused by an earthquake

READING NOTES

Social Studies Vocabulary

As you complete the Reading Notes, use these terms in your answers.

Han dynasty   bureaucracy   industry

Sections 1 to 7

If your class is doing the activity for this lesson, complete all of the Reading Notes for each section. *If your class is not doing the activity, skip the last part of each section.*

Section 1

1. How were the Han able to expand their empire? How far did it extend?

2. Describe three new military weapons used by the Han army.

3. On the tomb brick, quickly sketch and label the weapon that you think most strengthened the Han army. Then explain why you think this weapon was the most helpful.

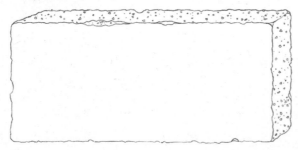

(Note: If your class is not doing the activity, skip the following.)

Follow the steps on Handout A to annotate the map below. Then answer the question below.

How did geography affect the expansion of the Han empire?

Map Title:

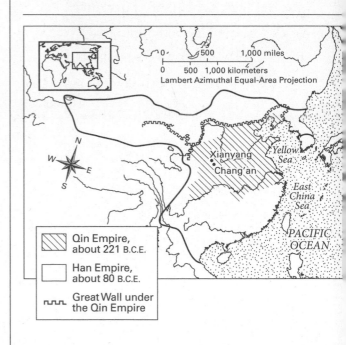

Qin Empire, about 221 B.C.E.

Han Empire, about 80 B.C.E.

Great Wall under the Qin Empire

© Teachers' Curriculum Institute

Section 2

1. How were Han dynasty rulers different from the Emperor of Qin?

2. Describe the Han government bureaucracy and tell how civil servants were hired and promoted.

3. On the tomb brick, quickly sketch and label the way you think the Han most improved Chinese government. Then explain why you chose this improvement.

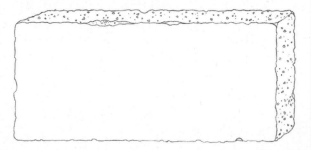

(Note: If your class is not doing the activity, skip the following.)

Explain why an exam for a government job should or should not contain questions like the ones on the exam you just took.

Section 3

1. What tasks and problems did Han farmers face?

2. Describe three agricultural tools that were invented during the Han period.

3. On the tomb brick, quickly sketch and label the tool you think most improved agriculture during the Han dynasty. Then explain why you chose this tool.

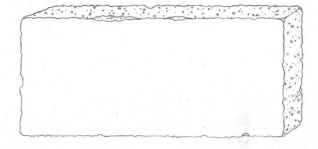

(Note: If your class is not doing the activity, skip the following.)

If you were a Han farmer, how would your life be different because of these agricultural inventions?

Section 4

1. How was the production of silk made easier during the Han period?

2. Why was salt an important trade item in ancient times?

3. On the tomb brick, quickly sketch and label the invention that you think most improved industry during the Han period. Then explain why you chose this invention.

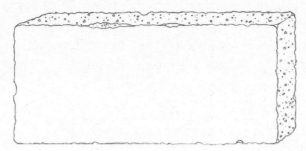

(Note: If your class is not doing the activity, skip the following.)

What parts of the Chinese drilling process do the glass of water, the straw, and the empty glass represent?

Section 5

1. Describe Chinese calligraphy writing.

2. Explain why paper was an improvement over earlier writing materials.

3. On the tomb brick, quickly sketch and label the use of paper you think was most important during the Han dynasty. Then explain why you chose this use.

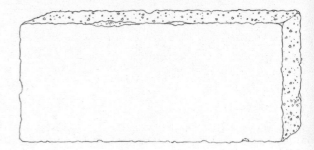

(Note: If your class is not doing the activity, skip the following.)

Why did your written character turn out better on paper than if you had used silk or a strip of bamboo?

© Teachers' Curriculum Institute

Section 6

1. What did the Han believe caused illness?

2. Fill in the matrix below to describe techniques used by traditional Chinese healers.

Technique	What Is It?	Why Is It Used?
Acupuncture		
Moxibustion		

3. List two discoveries made by Chinese doctors during the Han dynasty.

4. On the tomb brick, quickly sketch and label what you think was the most important achievement in the field of medicine during the Han period. Then explain why you chose this achievement.

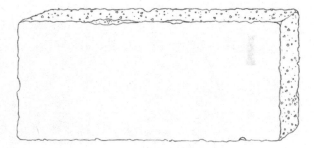

(Note: If your class is not doing the activity, skip the following.)

According to Chinese medicine, how can the technique you just learned about help relieve stress?

Section 7

1. What did Chinese astronomers discover?

2. For what purposes did the Chinese use the compass and the seismograph?

3. On the tomb brick, quickly sketch and label what you think was the most important advancement in the field of science during the Han dynasty. Then explain why you chose this discovery.

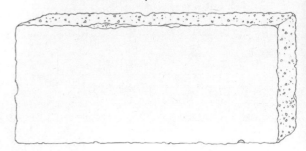

(Note: If your class is not doing the activity, skip the following.)

Follow the steps on Handout G to complete the horizontal bar graph below.

Title:

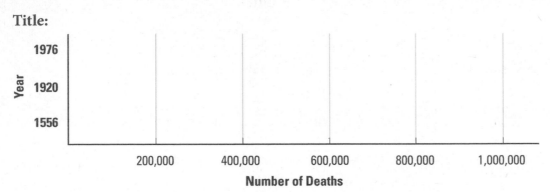

Why would the Chinese want to invent the seismograph?

PROCESSING

On a separate piece of paper, sketch these tomb bricks and headings. Make your sketches large enough to follow the directions below.

Han Government and Empire   People's Daily Lives

- In the first brick, draw and color an illustration of the achievement you think most contributed to the expansion of the Han empire. In a well-written paragraph under the brick, explain why you chose this achievement.

- In the second brick, draw and color an illustration of the achievement you think most improved the daily lives of people in China during the Han period. In a well-written paragraph under the brick, explain why you chose this achievement.

    © Teachers' Curriculum Institute

The Silk Road

How did the Silk Road promote an exchange of goods and ideas?

What is the origin of each item listed below? If you think that the item originated in the United States, place an *X* in that column. If you think that the item originated in another culture, place an *X* in that column.

Item	Originated in the United States	Originated in Another Culture
Chewing gum		
Yo-yo		
Chocolate		
Little Red Riding Hood		
Ice cream		
Shampoo		
Pasta		
Lipstick		
Fork		
Doughnut		
Roller skates		
Pancake		
Sandwich		
Paper		
Zipper		

READING NOTES

Social Studies Vocabulary

As you complete the Reading Notes, use these terms in your answers.

Silk Road   caravan
trade route   cultural diffusion

Section 1

1. Which Chinese empire opened the Silk Road? How did the empire do it?

2. List three things Zhang Qian brought back to China from his journeys.

3. What was China's most valuable trade good? Why? What product that was new to the Chinese did the Romans trade?

If your class is doing the activity for this lesson, complete the T-chart when you are asked to do so. *If your class is not doing the activity, skip the following.*

Trading Along the Silk Road

Classroom Experience	Historical Connection
• Students were allowed to move to only one trading center at a time.	• Traders had to travel long distances and then rest for days or weeks.
•	•
•	•
•	•
•	•
•	•
•	•

                                    © Teachers' Curriculum Institute

On this map, complete the four tasks listed below.

The Eastern Half of the Silk Road During the Han Dynasty

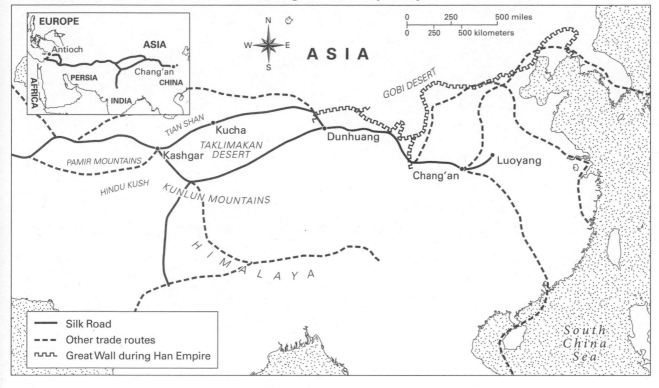

1. In appropriate locations along the route, draw two "warning signs" to represent the dangers of traveling the eastern part of the Silk Road.

2. Near Dunhuang, draw and label symbols for two valuable products from China that were traded on the Silk Road.

3. Near Kucha, draw and label symbols for two valuable products from Central Asia that were traded on the Silk Road.

4. Near Kashgar, draw and label symbols for two valuable products from India that were traded on the Silk Road.

Answer the following questions in complete sentences.

1. How did traders overcome the challenge of the desert?

2. Why was silk the perfect trading good?

On this map, complete the three tasks listed below.

The Western Half of the Silk Road During the Han Dynasty

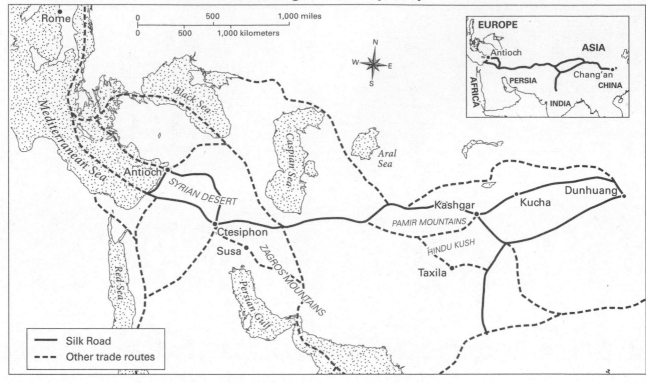

1. In appropriate locations along the route, draw two "warning signs" to represent the dangers of traveling the western part of the Silk Road.

2. Near Ctesiphon, draw and label symbols for two valuable products from Egypt, Arabia, and Persia that were traded on the Silk Road.

3. Near Antioch, draw and label symbols for two valuable products from Rome that were traded on the Silk Road.

Answer the following questions in complete sentences.

1. How were goods transported after they reached Antioch? Where were they sent?

2. Why did the Roman emperor forbid men from wearing silk?

© Teachers' Curriculum Institute

On this map, complete the three tasks listed below.

The Silk Road

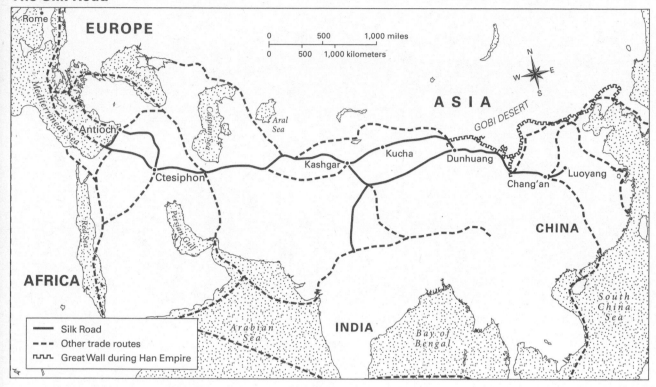

1. Near China, draw and label symbols for two foods or products that China learned about as a result of trade on the Silk Road.

2. Near Rome, draw and label symbols for two foods or products that the West learned about as a result of trade on the Silk Road.

3. Near India, draw and label a symbol for Buddhism. Then draw an arrow that shows how Buddhism spread from India to China.

Answer the following question in a complete sentence: *How did the Silk Road promote an exchange of goods and ideas?*

PROCESSING

Write a journal entry from the perspective of a trader on the Silk Road. Describe each of the following:

- where you traveled
- two dangers you encountered and how you overcame them
- two goods you traded and why
- one idea or belief you learned about

Sketch and label a simple illustration that represents your experience while traveling and trading along the Silk Road.

© Teachers' Curriculum Institute

INVESTIGATING PRIMARY SOURCES

Identifying and Evaluating Evidence

Use the reading to create a claim to answer this question: *How did the geography of the Silk Road affect travelers?*

Claim:

What evidence from the primary sources documents support your claim? Fill out the chart below. Circle the two strongest pieces of evidence.

Source	Evidence	How does this support the claim?

You can use this evidence to strengthen your claim. Write your revised claim below.

Constructing an Argument

Create an argument to answer the question: *How did the geography of the Silk Road affect travelers?* Your argument should:

- clearly state your claim.
- include evidence from multiple sources.
- provide explanations for how the sources support the claim.

Use this rubric to evaluate your argument. Make changes as needed.

Score	Description
3	The claim clearly answers the question. The argument uses evidence from two or more primary sources that strongly support the claim. The explanations accurately connect to the evidence and claim.
2	The claim answers the question. The argument uses evidence from one or more primary sources that support the claim. Some of the explanations connect to the evidence and claim.
1	The claim fails to answer the question. The argument lacks evidence from primary sources. Explanations are missing or are unrelated to the evidence and claim.

  © Teachers' Curriculum Institute

Timeline Skills

Analyze the Unit 4 timeline in the Student Text. Also think about what you have learned in this unit. Then answer the following questions.

1. Of the Han, Qin, and Shang dynasties, which was the first to rule? What area did they control?

2. During which dynasty was early Chinese writing placed on oracle bones?

3. How did the Zhou justify their rule?

4. About when did the Zhou dynasty end?

5. Did Confucius live before or after the first unification of China?

6. What did Emperor Qin Shi Huangdi accomplish?

7. For about how many years did the Han dynasty rule China?

8. Did expansion begin in the earlier or later half of the Han dynasty? To what regions did they expand?

9. How are the two events that took place in 138 B.C.E. and 65 C.E. related?

10. When was paper invented, and why was it important?

Critical Thinking

Use the timeline and the lessons in the unit to answer the following questions.

11. What are the main teachings of Confucianism, Daoism, and Legalism, and why did they develop during the Zhou dynasty?

12. Was Emperor Qin Shi Huangdi an effective emperor? Support your answer by describing at least one effective action and one ineffective action he took as emperor.

13. The Han dynasty improved the lives of people in China.
    a. What significant changes did the Han make in government?

    b. What is another important Han contribution that helped people?

14. If you could add three more events to this timeline, which ones would you choose? List each event and explain why you think it is important enough to add to the timeline.
    a.

    b.

    c.

    © Teachers' Curriculum Institute

UNIT **5**

Ancient Greece

Geography Challenge

Lesson 25: Geography and the Settlement of Greece
How did geography influence settlement and way of life in ancient Greece?

Lesson 26: The Rise of Democracy
How did democracy develop in ancient Greece?

Lesson 27: Life in Two City-States: Athens and Sparta
What were the major differences between Athens and Sparta?

Lesson 28: Fighting the Greco-Persian Wars
What factors influenced the outcome of the Greco-Persian wars?

Lesson 29: The Golden Age of Athens
What were the major cultural achievements of Athens?

Lesson 30: Alexander the Great and His Empire
How did Alexander build his empire?

Lesson 31: The Legacy of Ancient Greece
How did ancient Greece contribute to the modern world?

Timeline Challenge

Ancient Greece

GREECE

500 miles

500 kilometers

Lambert Azimuthal Equal-Area Projection

250

250

0

0

© Teachers' Curriculum Institute

Geography Skills

Analyze the maps in "Setting the Stage" for Unit 5 the Student Text. Then answer the following questions and fill out the map as directed.

1. Locate the sea that is south of ancient Greece. Label it.

    What sea lies along the eastern coast of Greece? Label it.

2. On what continent is ancient Greece located? Label it.

3. On which continents did the ancient Greeks establish settlements? On your map, shade these colonies and label the continents on which they are located.

4. Use the large map in the Student Text to name the peninsula in Europe that had Greek colonies that were the farthest away from mainland Greece. Then use the scale of miles on the map in the Student Text to measure the approximate distance from mainland Greece to this colony.

5. Locate the Adriatic and the Ionian seas on your map and label them. How did the seas surrounding ancient Greece influence its development?

6. In what direction would you travel to get from ancient Greece to Egypt?

7. Locate and label the cities of Athens and Sparta. Which one was farther north?

Critical Thinking

Answer the following questions in complete sentences.

8. Review the Unit 5 "Setting the Stage" feature in the Student Text. The Greeks did not have much level land for farming or grazing cattle. How did they meet this challenge?

9. Over time, as the population of ancient Greek communities increased, some communities did not have enough farmland to produce enough food for the population. Using the large map in the Unit 5 "Setting the Stage" feature, predict what ancient Greeks did to solve this problem.

10. Most of the Greek islands lie between the Greek mainland and Asia Minor (present-day Turkey). Would this fact have made travel to Asia Minor easier or more difficult? Explain your answer.

11. When the ancient Greeks established settlements in other countries, they came into contact with people from other cultures. How might this have affected the history of ancient Greece?

 © Teachers' Curriculum Institute

Geography and the Settlement of Greece

How did geography influence settlement and way of life in ancient Greece?

P R E V I E W

Examine the map and the information about the physical geography of Greece. Then answer the question that follows.

Facts About the Geography of Greece

- Greece has no major rivers.
- Greece is surrounded on three sides by seas.
- Greece is mostly mountainous.
- Greece includes hundreds of islands.

How do you think the physical geography of Greece influenced where people settled and how they lived?

Physical Features of the Greek Peninsula

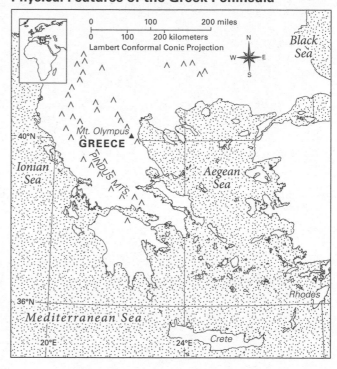

R E A D I N G   N O T E S

Social Studies Vocabulary

As you complete the Reading Notes, use these terms in your answers.

peninsula   Aegean Sea   colony

Section 1

1. Examine the map in Section 1 of the Student Text. Where did the ancient Greeks mostly settle?

2. Why were ancient Greek communities isolated from each other?

3. List three or more reasons why travel was challenging in ancient Greece.

   •

   •

   •

Section 2

1. Complete the chart by listing challenges facing Greek farmers in the first column, and the ways in which farmers met these challenges in the second column.

Challenges to Greek Farmers	How Farmers Met These Challenges

2. Why did some Greek settlements fight each other?

                                    © Teachers' Curriculum Institute

Section 3

1. What was the primary reason why the ancient Greeks started colonies?

2. Describe the actions that the ancient Greeks were likely to take when starting a new colony.

3. When did the Greeks establish colonies? Where were the colonies located?

Section 4

1. Why did some ancient Greek settlements trade?

2. What goods from the Greek mainland were traded? What goods did the Greeks get in exchange?

3. Identify two or more challenges merchant ships faced.

    •

    •

PROCESSING

Use the graphic organizer below to create a storyboard for a children's book about the geography of ancient Greece. A storyboard is a simple draft of your ideas.

In the title box, write a title for your children's book. In each of the page boxes, make a simple sketch and then write two or three sentences explaining the topic. For example, on *Page 2: Visiting a Farm,* you might sketch crops growing on a hillside, and write about what farmers grew and why. Make sure your sentences are appropriately written for a young audience.

Title:	
Page 1: Traveling from Place to Place	Page 2: Visiting a Farm
Page 3: Starting a Colony	Page 4: Sailing on a Merchant Ship

© Teachers' Curriculum Institute

The Rise of Democracy

How did democracy develop in ancient Greece?

PREVIEW

Suppose that you are on a sports team that is one play away from winning a game. Which of these options do you think is the best way to choose the final play of the game?

A. Have the coach or the assistant coach choose the final play.

B. Have the three most talented players choose the final play.

C. Have the most popular player choose the final play.

D. Have all the team members choose the final play.

In the space below, write your choice and explain the reasons for your choice.

READING NOTES

Social Studies Vocabulary

As you complete the Reading Notes, use these terms in your answers.

| monarchy | oligarchy | democracy | assembly |
| aristocrat | tyranny | citizen | |

1. Shade in the bar below the timeline to show approximately when most Greek city-states had monarchies. Label this period on the timeline, using a simple visual that represents a monarchy.

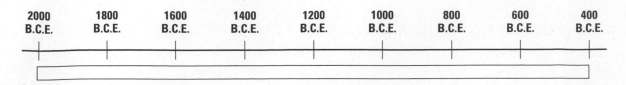

| 2000 B.C.E. | 1800 B.C.E. | 1600 B.C.E. | 1400 B.C.E. | 1200 B.C.E. | 1000 B.C.E. | 800 B.C.E. | 600 B.C.E. | 400 B.C.E. |

2. Under a monarchy, the power to make political decisions is in the hands of

_____ , usually called a _____ .

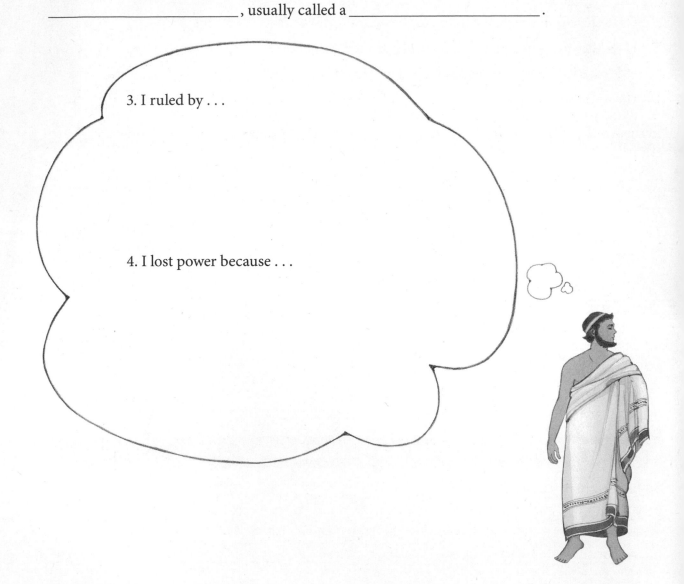

3. I ruled by . . .

4. I lost power because . . .

  © Teachers' Curriculum Institute

Section 2

1. Shade in the bar below the timeline to show approximately when most Greek city-states had oligarchies. Label this period on the timeline, using a simple visual that represents an oligarchy.

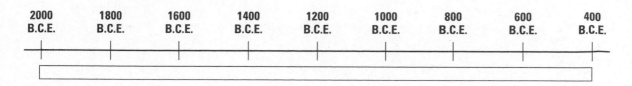

| 2000 B.C.E. | 1800 B.C.E. | 1600 B.C.E. | 1400 B.C.E. | 1200 B.C.E. | 1000 B.C.E. | 800 B.C.E. | 600 B.C.E. | 400 B.C.E. |

2. Under an oligarchy, the power to make political decisions is in the hands of _____, called _____ .

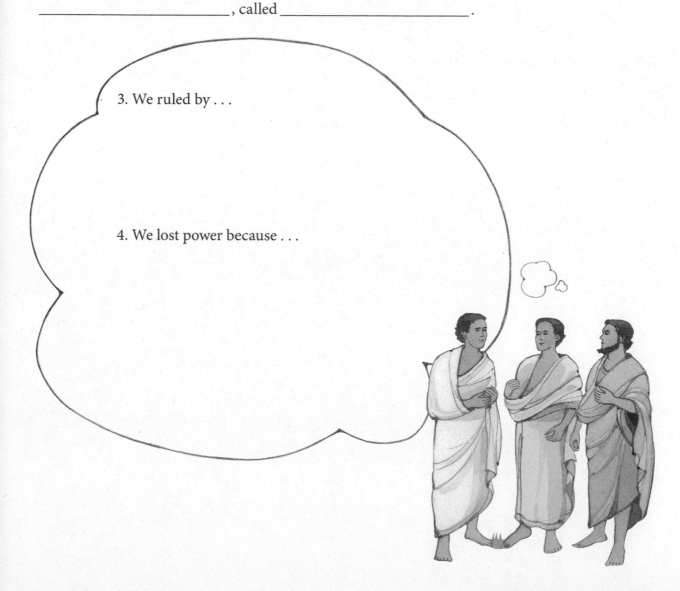

3. We ruled by . . .

4. We lost power because . . .

Section 3

1. Shade in the bar below the timeline to show approximately when most Greek
   city-states had tyrannies. Label this period on the timeline, using a simple
   visual that represents a tyranny.

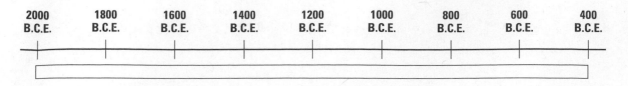

2000 B.C.E.	1800 B.C.E.	1600 B.C.E.	1400 B.C.E.	1200 B.C.E.	1000 B.C.E.	800 B.C.E.	600 B.C.E.	400 B.C.E.

2. Under a tyranny, the power to make political decisions is in the hands of
   _____ , called a _____ .

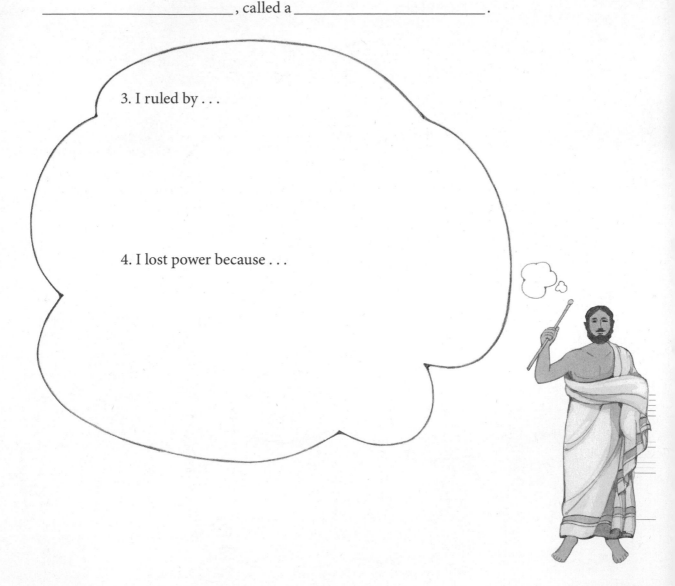

3. I ruled by . . .

4. I lost power because . . .

© Teachers' Curriculum Institute

1. Shade in the bar below the timeline to show approximately when Athens had a democracy. Label this period on the timeline, using a simple visual that represents a democracy.

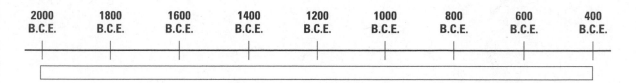

| 2000 B.C.E. | 1800 B.C.E. | 1600 B.C.E. | 1400 B.C.E. | 1200 B.C.E. | 1000 B.C.E. | 800 B.C.E. | 600 B.C.E. | 400 B.C.E. |

2. Under a democracy, the power to make political decisions is in the hands of
_____ , called _____ .

3. We ruled by . . .

4. Not all Greeks thought democracy was a good idea because . . .

PROCESSING

Complete the following report card to evaluate the four forms of government practiced in ancient Greece. For each form of government, write a grade for each of the topics listed at the top of the report card. Then answer the question at the bottom of the report card.

Key for Grades
A: Excellent
B: Very Good
C: Average
D: Poor
F: Fail

Report Card for Ancient Greek Governments

	Making Efficient Decisions	Giving Equality to All People	Meeting the Needs of the People
Monarchy			
Oligarchy			
Tyranny			
Democracy			

Which of the four forms of government do you think deserves the highest overall grade and why?

© Teachers' Curriculum Institute

Life in Two City-States: Athens and Sparta

What were the major differences between Athens and Sparta?

PREVIEW

Examine the two illustrations of ancient Greek city-states your teacher will show you. Then answer the questions below.

1. Describe the geography of the city-state in the top image. Do you think that this city-state was a farming or a trading community?

2. Describe the geography of the city-state in the bottom image. Do you think that this city-state was a farming or a trading community?

3. Using the details in the illustrations to help you, try to predict what other differences might have existed between these two city-states.

Social Studies Vocabulary

As you complete the Reading Notes, use these terms in your answers.

Athens	Peloponnesus	agora
Sparta	Council of 500	Council of Elders

Section 1

Athens and Sparta

1. On the map, circle the city-state of Athens.
2. Briefly describe Athens's location.

3. On the map, place a square around the city-state of Sparta.
4. Briefly describe Sparta's location.

© Teachers' Curriculum Institute

Section 2 to 9

If your class is doing the activity for this lesson, follow directions 1 through 3 below to complete your Reading Notes for Sections 2 to 9. *(Note: If your class is not doing the activity, follow only directions 1 and 2 below.)*

1. For each topic below, read the appropriate sections in the lesson.

2. Write three or more key details to answer the section questions.

3. Answer the challenge questions and check the answer key.

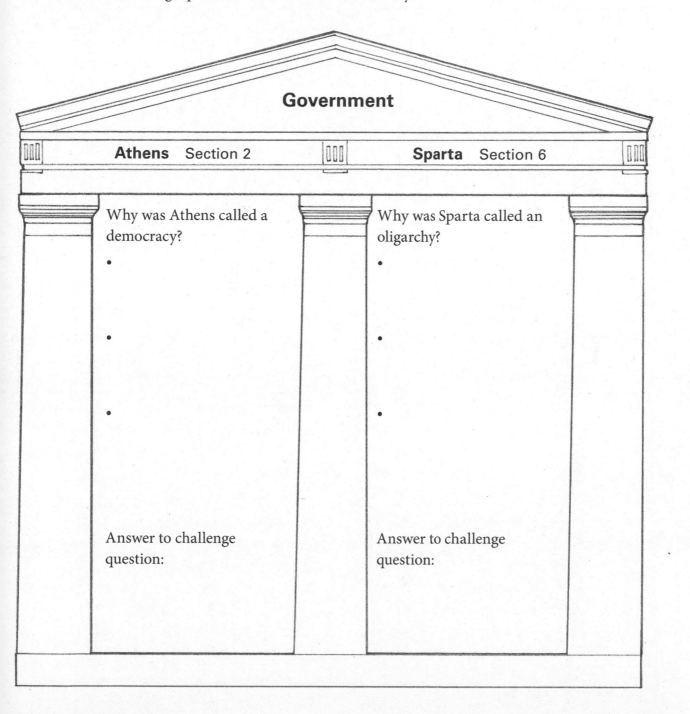

Government

Athens Section 2

Why was Athens called a democracy?

-
-
-

Answer to challenge question:

Sparta Section 6

Why was Sparta called an oligarchy?

-
-
-

Answer to challenge question:

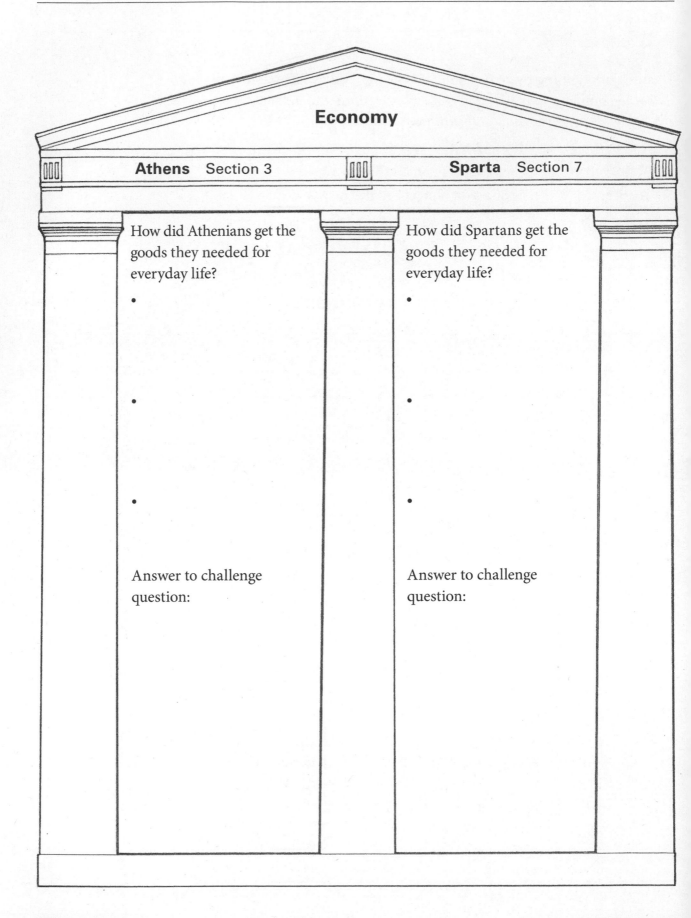

Economy

Athens Section 3

Sparta Section 7

How did Athenians get the goods they needed for everyday life?

-
-
-

Answer to challenge question:

How did Spartans get the goods they needed for everyday life?

-
-
-

Answer to challenge question:

© Teachers' Curriculum Institute

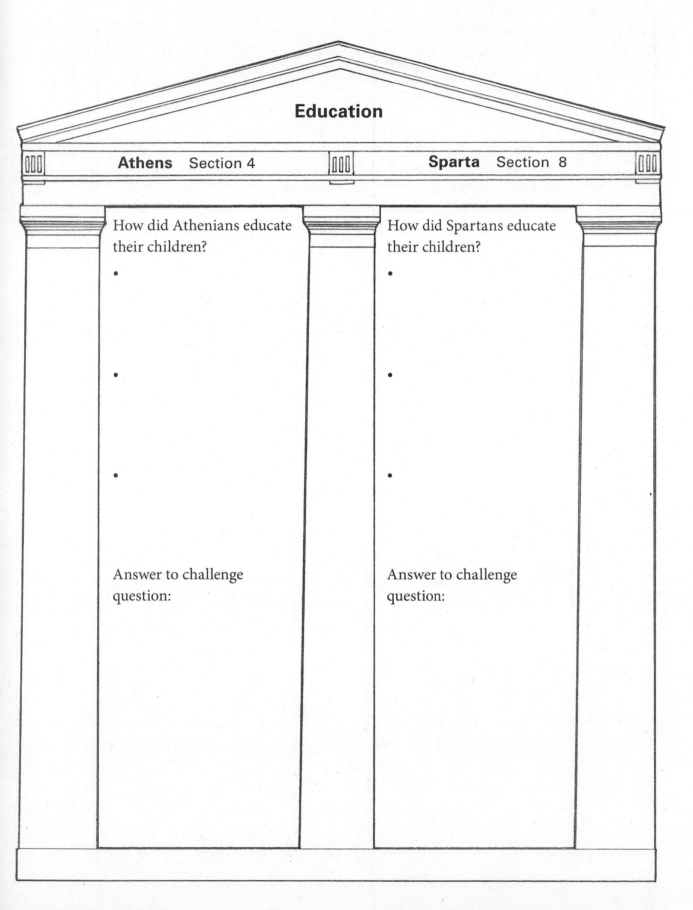

Education

Athens Section 4

Sparta Section 8

How did Athenians educate
their children?

-
-
-

How did Spartans educate
their children?

-
-
-

Answer to challenge
question:

Answer to challenge
question:

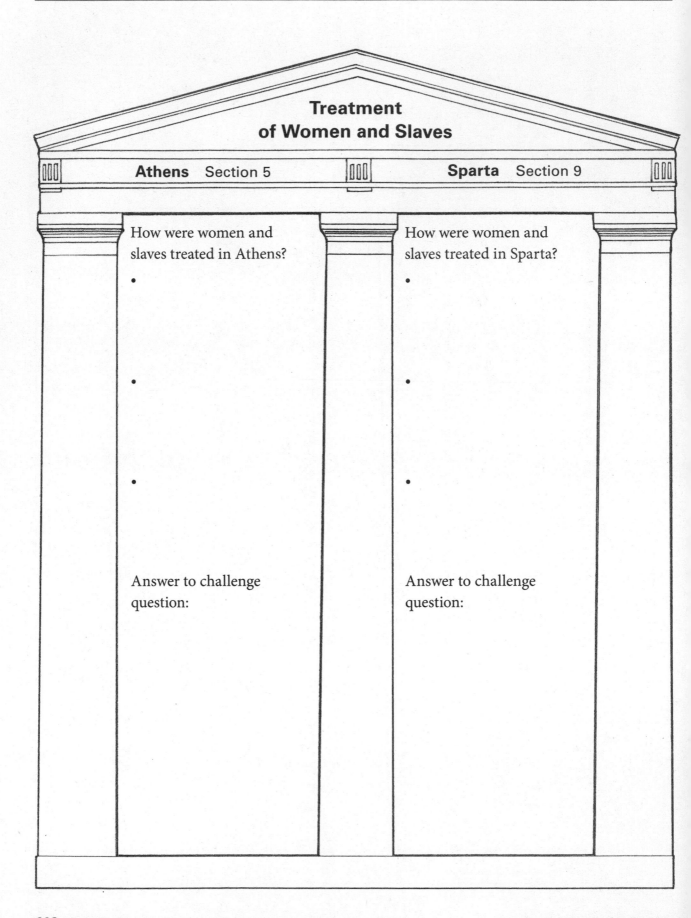

**Treatment
of Women and Slaves**

Athens Section 5 | **Sparta** Section 9

How were women and
slaves treated in Athens?

-
-
-

Answer to challenge
question:

How were women and
slaves treated in Sparta?

-
-
-

Answer to challenge
question:

© Teachers' Curriculum Institute

PROCESSING

Compare and contrast the city-states of Athens and Sparta by completing the chart below with sentences each face might say. Your statements should highlight major similarities and differences between the two city-states, in the areas of government, economy, education, and the treatment of women and slaves.

- For the Athenian citizen at the left, write four or more statements in the left column that describe what life was like in Athens. For example, you might write, "In Athens, all citizens participate in the government by voting on laws."

- For the Spartan soldier at the right, write four or more statements in the right column that describe what life was like in Sparta. For example, you might write, "In Sparta, both boys and girls receive military training from the age of 7."

Fighting the Greco-Persian Wars

What factors influenced the outcome of the Greco-Persian Wars?

Silently read the excerpt from a primary source below. The play describes the events that took place during one of the battles of the Greco-Persian Wars. Use what you've read to answer the questions below.

A Greek Play

Excerpt from *The Persians*

by Aeschylus

Messenger: Know then, in numbers the barbaric fleet
Was far superior: in ten squadrons, each
Of thirty ships, Greece plough'd the deep; of these
One held a distant station. Xerxes led
A thousand ships; their number well I know;
Two hundred more, and seven, that swept the seas
With speediest sail: this was their full amount.
And in the engagement seem'd we not secure
Of victory? But unequal fortune sunk
Our scale in fight, discomfiting our host.

• What imagery can you find in this primary source excerpt?

• What do the header, title, and author reveal about this piece?

• Does knowing the author's background reveal any possible biases he may have?

• How can historians supplement works like this one?

Social Studies Vocabulary

As you complete the Reading Notes, use these terms in your answers.

| Persian Empire | Hellespont | Greco-Persian wars |
| Darius | Xerxes | cavalry |

Section 1

1. Color in the Persian Empire on the map and key below. Then use a different color for Greece.

The Persian Empire

2. How did the Persians build their empire?

3. How did King Darius rule the Persian Empire?

Section 2

What happened during the Ionian Revolt, and why was it important?

© Teachers' Curriculum Institute

Section 3

1. Summarize what happened at the Battle of Marathon.

2. Draw and label a simple illustration or symbol that shows why the battle was important.

3. Circle the factor that you think **best** explains why the Greeks won the Battle of Marathon. Then write one or two sentences explaining your choice.

    A. They were joined together as allies.

    B. They had better fighting equipment.

    C. They knew the geography of the area.

    D. They used clever military strategy.

1. Summarize what happened at the Battle of Thermopylae.

2. Draw and label a simple illustration or symbol that shows why the battle was important.

3. Circle the factor that you think **best** explains why the Persians won the Battle of Thermopylae. Then write one or two sentences explaining your choice.

   A. They were joined together as allies.

   B. They had better fighting equipment.

   C. They knew the geography of the area.

   D. They used clever military strategy.

© Teachers' Curriculum Institute

Section 5

1. Summarize what happened at the Battle of Salamis.

2. Draw and label a simple illustration or symbol that shows why the battle was important.

3. Circle the factor that you think **best** explains why the Greeks won the Battle of Salamis. Then write one or two sentences explaining your choice.

   A. They were joined together as allies.

   B. They had better fighting equipment.

   C. They knew the geography of the area.

   D. They used clever military strategy.

1. Summarize what happened at the Battle of Plataea.

2. Draw and label a simple illustration or symbol that shows why the battle was important.

3. Circle the factor that you think **best** explains why the Greeks won the Battle of Plataea. Then write one or two sentences explaining your choice.

   A. They were joined together as allies.   B. They had better fighting equipment.

   C. They knew the geography of the area.   D. They used clever military strategy.

PROCESSING

Listed below are four factors that contributed to a Greek victory in the Greco-Persian wars. On the lines next to the letters, rank these factors from the most important (1) to the least important (4).

_____ A. The Greeks were joined together as allies.

_____ B. The Greeks had better fighting equipment.

_____ C. The Greeks knew the geography of the area.

_____ D. The Greeks used clever military strategy.

On a separate piece of paper, write a paragraph justifying your choice for the most important factor.

                    © Teachers' Curriculum Institute

The Golden Age of Athens

What were the major cultural achievements of Athens?

In Athens, public funerals were held for soldiers who had died in battle. In 430 B.C.E., after a difficult year of war, an Athenian leader named Pericles spoke at such a funeral. In his speech, he described the greatness of Athens and why it was important to keep on fighting. Below is an excerpt from that speech.

Carefully read the excerpt and then answer the questions that follow.

> . . . we have not forgotten to provide for our weary [tired] spirits many relaxations from toil [hard work]; we have regular games and sacrifices throughout the year; our homes are beautiful and elegant; and the delight which we daily feel in all these things helps to banish [send away] sorrow. Because of the greatness of our city, the fruits of the whole earth flow in upon us; so that we enjoy the goods of other countries as freely as our own. . . . To sum up: I say that Athens is the school of Hellas [Greece]. . . . Such is the city for whose sake these men nobly fought and died. . . .
>
> — Pericles, Funeral Oration, in *History of the Peloponnesian War* by Thucydides.

1. According to Pericles, what made Athens great?

2. What else have you learned about Athens that might make people think of it as a great city?

3. Why do you think Pericles would call Athens the "school of Greece"?

READING NOTES

Social Studies Vocabulary

As you complete the Reading Notes, use these terms in your answers.

Pericles	myth	Socrates
Parthenon	drama	Panathenaic Games
acropolis		

Section 1

1. What contributions did Pericles make to Athens after the Greco-Persian wars?

2. Why can Athens be called a city of contrasts?

Sections 2 to 7

As you begin each section of the Reading Notes, locate the related site on the map of Athens below. Then answer the questions for that section.

Athens, 479–431 B.C.E.

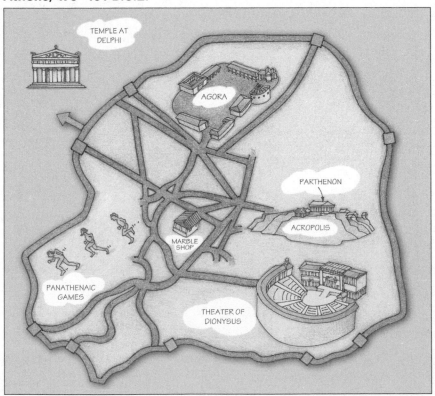

© Teachers' Curriculum Institute

Section 2

The Site: You are visiting the Temple of Apollo at Delphi, a town outside Athens, to learn about religion.

1. Why would a person go to see an oracle?

2. What did the ancient Greeks believe about where gods and goddesses lived and what they were like?

3. In what ways was religion a part of the everyday lives of the ancient Greeks?

Section 3

The Site: You are standing among the grand temples on the acropolis in Athens to learn about architecture.

1. Why did the ancient Greeks build temples like the Parthenon?

2. Identify the three types of Greek columns and describe one characteristic of each.

3. What features made the Parthenon one of the most beautiful temples in ancient Greece?

Section 4

The Site: You are visiting a marble workshop to learn about sculpture.

1. How did the styles of ancient Egyptian statues influence those of the ancient Greeks?

2. How did styles of Greek sculpture change over time?

3. Who was Phidias, and what did he do?

Section 5

The Site: You are visiting the Theater of Dionysus to learn about drama.

1. How many people could a theater hold, and how might its shape help a large audience?

2. Identify two ways in which ancient Greek drama differed from modern plays and movies.

    © Teachers' Curriculum Institute

Section 6

The Site: You are standing in the agora in Athens to learn about philosophy.

1. What did Greek philosophers do?

2. How did Socrates try to teach others?

3. What happened to Socrates?

Section 7

The Site: You are watching the Panathenaic Games, a series of athletic competitions, to learn about sports.

1. What was the purpose of the Panathenaic Games?

2. What events were held as part of the Panathenaic Games?

3. Identify one event that is still part of athletic competitions today, and then one event that is not.

In the space below, write a paragraph that answers the Essential Question:
What were the major cultural achievements of Athens?

In your paragraph, identify and describe at least three specific examples from
your Reading Notes.

© Teachers' Curriculum Institute

INVESTIGATING PRIMARY SOURCES

Identifying Evidence

Consider this question: *What do dramas of ancient Greece reveal about its society?*

Examine the four primary sources in the reading, and write down evidence from each source that helps answer this question.

Primary Source 1	Primary Source 2
Primary Source 3	**Primary Source 4**

Use the evidence you gathered to make a claim to the question.

Claim:

Constructing an Argument

Create an argument to answer the question: *What do dramas of ancient Greece reveal about its society?* Your argument should:

- clearly state your claim.
- include evidence from multiple sources.
- provide explanations for how the sources support the claim.

Use this rubric to evaluate your argument. Make changes as needed.

Score	Description
3	The claim clearly answers the question. The argument uses evidence from two or more primary sources that strongly support the claim. The explanations accurately connect to the evidence and claim.
2	The claim answers the question. The argument uses evidence from one or more primary sources that support the claim. Some of the explanations connect to the evidence and claim.
1	The claim fails to answer the question. The argument lacks evidence from primary sources. Explanations are missing or are unrelated to the evidence and claim.

  © Teachers' Curriculum Institute

Alexander the Great and His Empire

How did Alexander build his empire?

Throughout history, some rulers have been given the title "Great." For example, Ramses II of Egypt is also known as "Ramses the Great." Why do you think a ruler from ancient times would be given this title? In the space below, list at least three possible reasons.

A great ruler . . .

A great ruler . . .

A great ruler . . .

READING NOTES

Social Studies Vocabulary

As you complete the Reading Notes, use these terms in your answers.

Peloponnesian War	Aristotle	custom
Macedonia	Alexander the Great	Alexandria

Complete the boxes below the timeline. Name the event for each year and add a simple visual. Then, write complete sentences to answer the questions that follow.

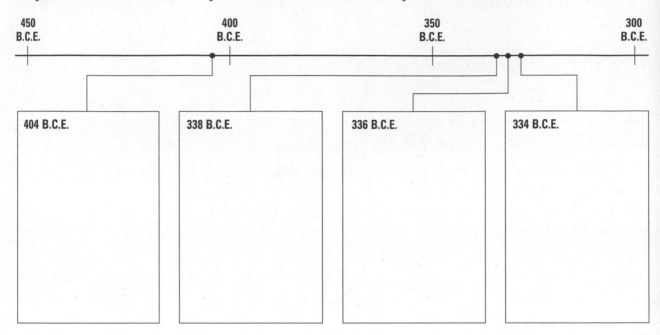

| 450 B.C.E. | 400 B.C.E. | 350 B.C.E. | 300 B.C.E. |

404 B.C.E.

338 B.C.E.

336 B.C.E.

334 B.C.E.

What roles did Athens and Sparta play in the Peloponnesian War?

Why was Alexander well trained to be a leader?

How did the Peloponnesian War contribute to the expansion of Macedonia?

How did Alexander plan to build his empire?

© Teachers' Curriculum Institute

Follow the directions to complete the map.

1. Shade in Alexander's empire on the map and in the key.

2. Circle the names of at least two regions or empires included in
    Alexander's empire.

3. Write a caption below the map that explains what is significant about
    the empire's size and what problems that size might create.

Alexander the Great's Empire, About 323 B.C.E.

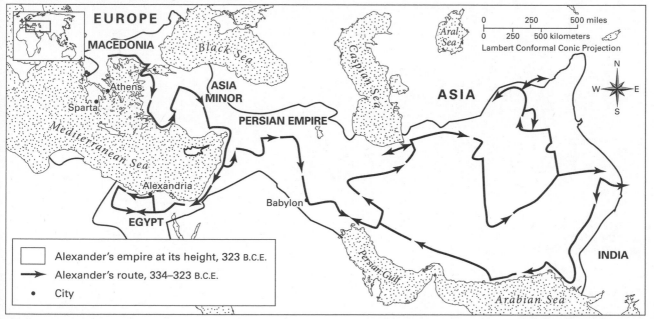

Section 4

Write three examples of how Alexander spread Greek ideas to unite the different peoples of his empire.

Section 5

Write three examples of how Alexander used religion to unite his empire.

© Teachers' Curriculum Institute

Write three examples of how Alexander adopted the ways of other cultures to show respect for the people he had conquered.

Write three or four sentences that explain what happened to Alexander's empire after he died.

PROCESSING

Design three medallions to show the different ways in which Alexander planned to build and unite his empire. For each medallion, include the following:

- A simple illustration.

- A corresponding title for Alexander (for example, "Alexander the Conqueror" or "Alexander the Religious"). You may **not** use "Alexander the Great."

- A caption. Briefly describe the illustration and explain how it shows one part of Alexander's plan to build and unite his empire.

Then choose the medallion that you think best demonstrates why Alexander is known as "Alexander the Great." Draw or color a decorative border around that medallion and explain why you chose it.

© Teachers' Curriculum Institute

The Legacy of Ancient Greece

How did ancient Greece contribute to the modern world?

Many English words have Greek roots. For example, the word *telephone* is made up of the Greek words *tel*, meaning "far off," and *phone*, meaning "voice." Use the key of Greek words to help you match the English terms below to their definitions.

_____ *autocracy*

_____ *autograph*

_____ *chronic*

_____ *chronology*

_____ *geology*

_____ *geothermal*

_____ *thermograph*

_____ *thermometer*

A. rule by one person

B. study of the order in time

C. an instrument for measuring temperature

D. study of the structure of Earth

E. relating to Earth's heat

F. somebody's signature

G. lasting over a long period of time

H. an instrument that records temperature

Key of Greek Words

Greek Word	Meaning
auto	self
chronos	time
geo	earth
grapho	draw, record, or write
kratos	power or rule
metron	measure
logy	study
thermo	heat

Social Studies Vocabulary

As you complete the Reading Notes, use these terms in your answers.

geometry   latitude   longitude   biology

If your class is doing the activity for this lesson, complete all three columns in the matrix below to complete your Reading Notes for Sections 1 to 10. *(Note: If your class is not doing the activity, skip the Placard Letter column.)*

Complete the matrix for each section. Write the placard letter that matches the legacy card. Draw and label a picture of the contribution that you think is most important today. List at least two other contributions in the reading.

	Placard Letter	Draw and Label the Most Important Contribution	List Other Contributions
Section 1 Literature and History			
Section 2 Government			
Section 3 Medicine			
Section 4 Mathematics			

© Teachers' Curriculum Institute

	Placard Letter	Draw and Label the Most Important Contribution	List Other Contributions
Section 5 Astronomy			
Section 6 Geography			
Section 7 Biology			
Section 8 Architecture			
Section 9 Theater			
Section 10 Sports			

© Teachers' Curriculum Institute

PROCESSING

Along the spectrum from least to most significant, consider the impact on life today of the contributions that ancient Greeks made in each of these areas:

Literature and History	Mathematics	Biology	Theater
Government	Astronomy	Architecture	Sports
Medicine	Geography		

Choose five items from the list above to place along your spectrum. For each item you choose, do the following:

- Label the spectrum.
- Draw an appropriate symbol or illustration.
- Below the drawing, write one sentence explaining your placement.

**Most Significant Impact
on Modern Life**

**Least Significant Impact
on Modern Life**

© Teachers' Curriculum Institute

Preparing to Write: Listing Reasons for Opposing Points of View

In 1986, the owner of a television network bought the rights to more than 100 old black-and-white movies. His company reedited them in color so that the films would have more appeal to modern viewers. While some professionals in the movie industry were not bothered by his actions, many more were outraged. It was the standard of the 1930s and 1940s to film in black and white, critics said. These films were the creations of the directors. To change the movies was to tamper with art and history. Directors, including some whose movies were among those being changed, called the colorizers "fools," and their actions "criminal." One director called it "the death knell of an entire art form."

Suppose that the sculptors of ancient Greece could see how Vinzenz Brinkmann has attempted to reconstruct their work. Do you think that they would approve or object to modern archaeologists adding color to their sculptures? List reasons why you think ancient Greek sculptors might have each of these points of view.

Adding Color to Ancient Sculptures

Reasons to Approve	Reasons to Object

Writing a Point-of-View Paragraph

Suppose that you are a sculptor from ancient Greece. Would you approve of or object to the Brinkmanns' replicas, or copies, of your work in color? Write a paragraph expressing and explaining your point of view. Support your position, using ideas from the chart you completed on the preceding page and information from the Reading Further.

Use this rubric to evaluate your paragraph. Make changes to your work if you need to.

Score	Description
3	The paragraph clearly states a position. Very relevant statements and facts support the position. There are no spelling or grammar errors.
2	The paragraph states a position. Somewhat relevant statements and facts support the position. There are some spelling or grammar errors.
1	The paragraph does not state a position. There are few or no statements and facts to support a position. There are many spelling or grammar errors.

© Teachers' Curriculum Institute

Timeline Skills

Analyze the Unit 5 timeline in the Student Text. Also think about what you have learned in this unit. Then answer the following questions.

1. By about what year were Greek city-states flourishing?

2. Of democracy, oligarchy, and tyranny, which form of government was first used in Greece?

3. About how many years after the development of oligarchies did democracy appear?

4. Where did democracy develop? About when did that happen?

5. Did the Golden Age of Athens happen before or after the Greco-Persian Wars?

6. The Golden Age ends at the same time as another event begins. What is this event, and why might it have contributed to the end of the Golden Age?

7. During which war did Pericles deliver his Funeral Oration speech?

8. Was Alexander the Great tutored by the Greek philosopher Socrates? How do you know?

9. What did Alexander the Great accomplish?

10. Who was Euclid, and why is he important?

Critical Thinking

Use the timeline and the lessons in the unit to answer the following questions.

11. Democracy is a form of government that developed from earlier forms of government and continued to change over time.

    a. What were the earlier forms of government, and what were their disadvantages?

    b. How does the democracy of ancient Greece compare with that of the United States? Identify one similarity and one difference.

12. Compare and contrast the city-states of Athens and Sparta. How are they similar, and how are they different?

13. Identify an important ancient Greek figure in the arts and sciences that you think made the most significant contribution and explain your choice.

14. If you could add three more events to this timeline, which ones would you choose? List each event and explain why you think it is important enough to add to the timeline.

    a.

    b.

    c.

© Teachers' Curriculum Institute,

Ancient Rome

Geography Challenge

Lesson 32: Geography and the Early Development of Rome
How did the Etruscans and Greeks influence the development of Rome?

Lesson 33: The Rise of the Roman Republic
What were the characteristics of the Roman Republic, and how did they change over time?

Lesson 34: From Republic to Empire
Did the benefits of Roman expansion outweigh the costs?

Lesson 35: Daily Life in the Roman Empire
How did wealth affect daily life in the Roman Empire?

Lesson 36: The Origins and Spread of Christianity
How did Christianity originate and spread?

Lesson 37: Learning About World Religions: Christianity
How do the beliefs and practices of Christianity shape Christian lives?

Lesson 38: The Legacy of Rome in the Modern World
To what extent does ancient Rome influence us today?

Timeline Challenge

The Roman Empire, About 117 C.E.

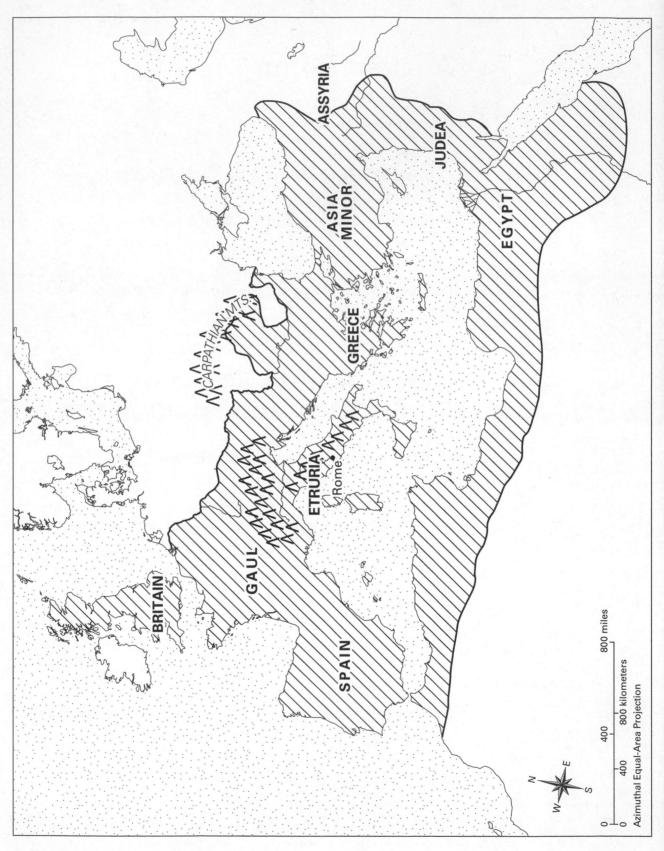

ASSYRIA

JUDEA

ASIA MINOR

EGYPT

CARPATHIAN MTS.

GREECE

ETRURIA

Rome

GAUL

BRITAIN

SPAIN

N
E
S
W

Azimuthal Equal-Area Projection

0   400   800 miles

0   400   800 kilometers

© Teachers' Curriculum Institute

Geography Skills

Analyze the maps in "Setting the Stage" for Unit 6 in the Student Text. Then answer the following questions and fill out the map as directed.

1. Locate the Alps. Label them.

2. What mountain range runs the length of the Italian peninsula? Label it.

3. Locate Rome. On what river is it located? Label this river.

4. What is a peninsula? Label the seas that make Italy a peninsula.

5. Locate the Po River. Label it. Use the compass rose to determine the answer to the following questions: In what direction does the Po River run? In what direction does the Tiber River run? How might the Tiber River have been helpful to the development of Rome?

6. Look at the map of the Roman Empire, displayed in the Unit 6 "Setting the Stage" feature in the Student Text. How far north did it extend? In Europe, how far west?

7. What physical feature formed the southern boundary of the Roman Empire? Label this feature.

Critical Thinking

Answer the following questions in complete sentences.

8. Consider the location of the Italian peninsula. How might this location have helped the Romans control trade in the Mediterranean region?

9. How might the mountain ranges of Italy have affected people's lives in ancient times?

10. Were the Romans more likely to choose a land or a water route to Spain? Explain your answer.

11. At one time, the Romans avoided sea travel because the Italian peninsula had few good harbors. What evidence can you find to support the argument that this geographical drawback was eventually overcome?

© Teachers' Curriculum Institute

Geography and the Early Development of Rome

How did the Etruscans and Greeks influence the development of Rome?

PREVIEW

Examine the two images of ancient Greek and Roman life. Circle and label three features that you see in both images.

Ancient Greece

Ancient Rome

Explain why you think these features are found in both ancient Greece and ancient Rome.

READING NOTES

Social Studies Vocabulary

As you complete the Reading Notes, use these terms in your answers.

Rome	cuniculus	Greco-Roman
Etruscan	gladiator	

Section 1

In the boxes below, create two simple cartoons. The first one should illustrate the myth of how Rome was founded. The second one should illustrate the history of how Rome was founded. To explain each cartoon, write a simple caption.

According to Myth

Caption:

According to History

Caption:

© Teachers' Curriculum Institute

Sections 2 to 7

For Sections 2 to 7, first read that section of the Student Text. In the box for that section, summarize the Etruscan or Greek influence on Rome. Then draw and label an arrow on the map to show how the influence came to Rome. An example has been done for you on the map.

Italian Peninsula, 6th Century B.C.E.

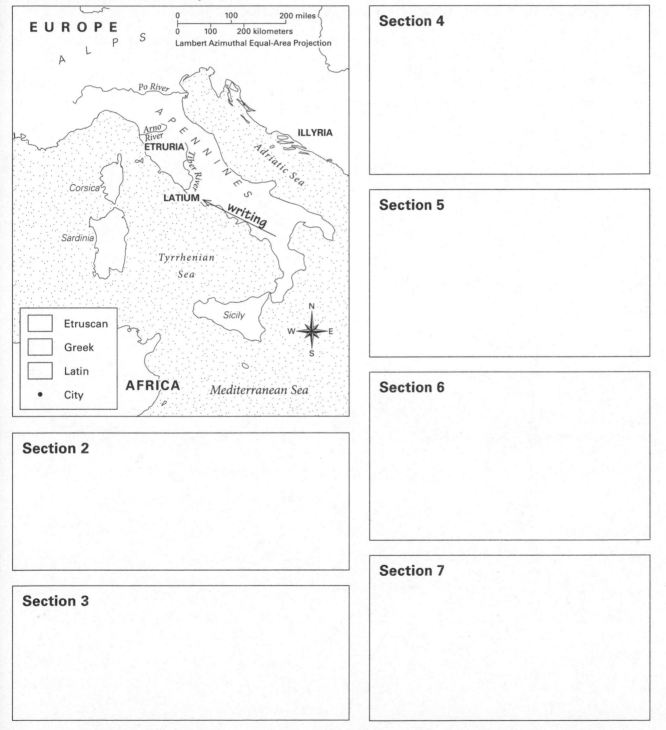

Section 4

Section 5

Section 6

Section 7

Section 2

Section 3

PROCESSING

Which two Etruscan or Greek influences had the biggest impact on Roman life? In the circles below, create coins that commemorate the two cultural influences you think were the most important.

Each coin should have:

- a drawing representing an Etruscan or a Greek influence, such as an arch or a column.
- a brief caption that describes the influence.
- a sentence that tells why you think each influence was so important to Roman life.

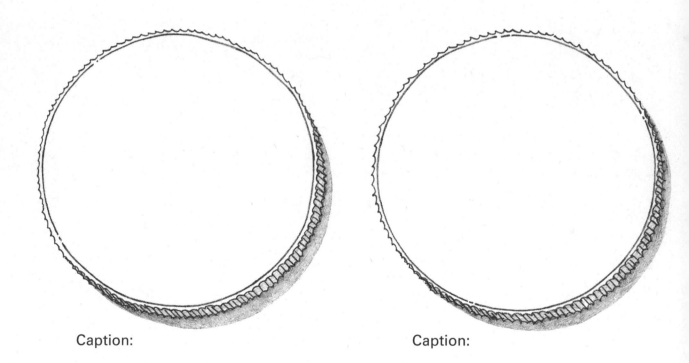

Caption: Caption:

        © Teachers' Curriculum Institute

The Rise of the Roman Republic

What were the characteristics of the Roman Republic, and how did they change over time?

PREVIEW

Describe a time when you felt you were treated unfairly. What actions did you take to improve the situation? What actions could you have taken that you didn't? Why didn't you?

READING NOTES

Social Studies Vocabulary

As you complete the Reading Notes, use these terms in your answers.

patrician	Senate	veto
plebian	consul	constitution
republic	tribune	

Section 1

1. Who ruled Rome between 616 and 509 B.C.E.?

2. Who were the patricians? How much power did they have?

3. Who were the plebeians? How much power did they have?

For each section, make a drawing on each pan of the balance scale to show how power was divided in early Rome. The drawing representing the group with more power should be on the "weighted," or lower, pan. Then answer the questions.

Section 2

1. On each pan of the balance, draw and label a stick figure to represent a patrician and a plebeian. Give them appropriate facial expressions.

2. What was the balance of power between patricians and plebeians when the republic was first created?

3. Why was the balance of power like this?

Section 3

1. On each pan of the balance, draw and label a stick figure to represent a patrician and a plebeian at the time described in this section. Give them appropriate facial expressions.

2. What was the balance of political power between patricians and plebeians during the Conflict of the Orders in 494 B.C.E.?

3. Why were the patricians frightened by the actions of the plebeians?

   © Teachers' Curriculum Institute

Section 4

1. Describe two ways in which plebeians gained more political power after the revolts of 494 B.C.E.

2. In each "step" below, summarize the change in Roman government that led to greater equality for the plebeians.

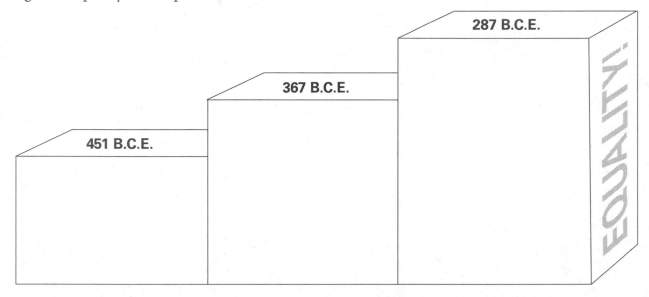

451 B.C.E.

367 B.C.E.

287 B.C.E.

EQUALITY!

3. On the spoke diagram below, add the political characteristics of the Roman Republic that were adopted later in other parts of the world.

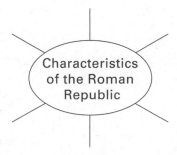

Characteristics of the Roman Republic

PROCESSING

Create an illustrated timeline to show how the characteristics of the Roman Republic changed over time. Include the following:

- the title "Rise of the Roman Republic"
- these dates: 616 B.C.E., 509 B.C.E., 494 B.C.E., 451 B.C.E., 287 B.C.E.
- a one-sentence summary for each date, explaining how the event changed government in the Roman Republic
- a simple illustration or symbol for each date

Use your timeline to answer the following question in a well-written paragraph: *Which change do you think was the most important, and why?*

© Teachers' Curriculum Institute

LESSON

34

From Republic to Empire

Did the benefits of Roman expansion outweigh the costs?

PREVIEW

Suppose that your family were much larger—perhaps two or three times larger than it is now. What would be some of the benefits of living in a larger family? What might be some of the drawbacks, or costs? Complete the T-chart below.

Benefits of a Larger Family	Costs of a Larger Family

READING NOTES

Social Studies Vocabulary

As you complete the Reading Notes, use these terms in your answers.

civil war	Punic Wars	Caesar Augustus
dictator	Julius Caesar	Pax Romana

© Teachers' Curriculum Institute

In the flowchart below, summarize the expansion of Rome during each
time period.

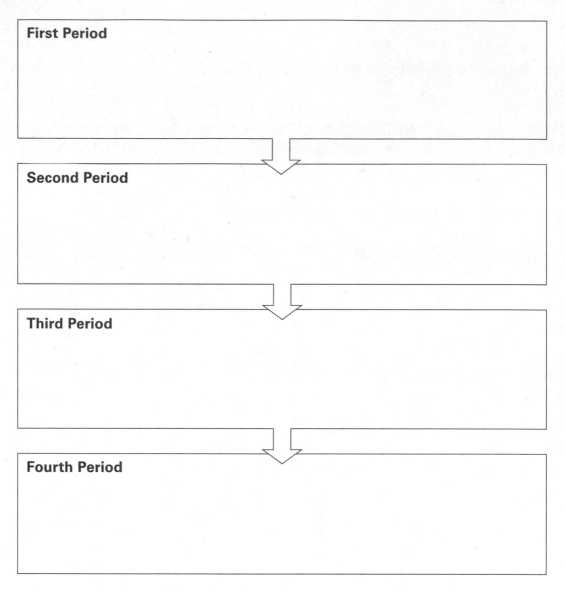

First Period

Second Period

Third Period

Fourth Period

Sections 2 to 5

As you read each section, complete these steps:

- Shade in the appropriate area of the map *Roman Territory, 509 B.C.E. to 14 C.E.*
  in a new color to show each Roman expansion. Color in the key to match.

- Find the corresponding section in the Reading Notes that follow the map.
  Outline the matching Roman column with the color you used on the map.

- In the Roman column, fill in the missing dates and answer the questions.

© Teachers' Curriculum Institute

Roman Territory, 509 B.C.E. to 14 C.E.

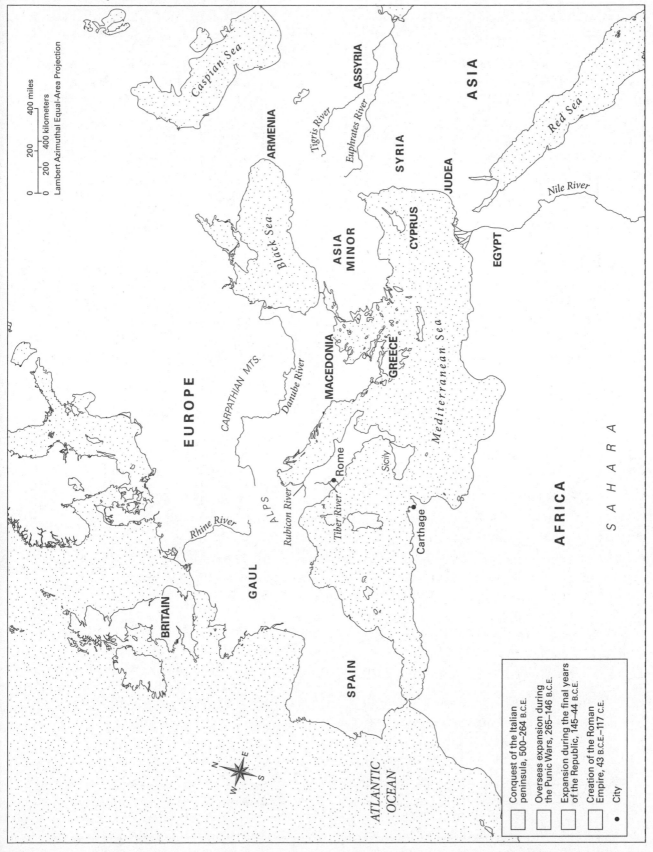

400 miles

200

0

400 kilometers

200

0

Lambert Azimuthal Equal-Area Projection

Caspian Sea

ASSYRIA

ASIA

ARMENIA

Tigris River

Euphrates River

SYRIA

Red Sea

JUDEA

Nile River

Black Sea

ASIA MINOR

CYPRUS

EGYPT

CARPATHIAN MTS.

EUROPE

Danube River

MACEDONIA

GREECE

Mediterranean Sea

Rhine River

ALPS

Rubicon River

Rome

Sicily

Tiber River

Carthage

SAHARA

AFRICA

GAUL

BRITAIN

SPAIN

ATLANTIC OCEAN

N
E
S
W

Conquest of the Italian peninsula, 500–264 B.C.E.

Overseas expansion during the Punic Wars, 265–146 B.C.E.

Expansion during the final years of the Republic, 145–44 B.C.E.

Creation of the Roman Empire, 43 B.C.E.–117 C.E.

• City

© Teachers' Curriculum Institute

Section 2

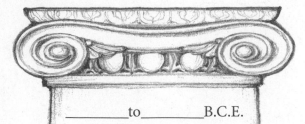

_____to_____B.C.E.

1. How were the Romans able to take control of the Italian peninsula?

2. Who might have had a negative view of Roman expansion during this period, and why?

Section 3

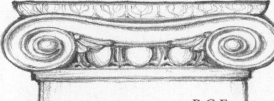

_____to_____B.C.E.

1. Why did Romans fight the Punic Wars? What did they gain?

2. Who might have had a negative view of Roman expansion during this period, and why?

© Teachers' Curriculum Institute

Section 4

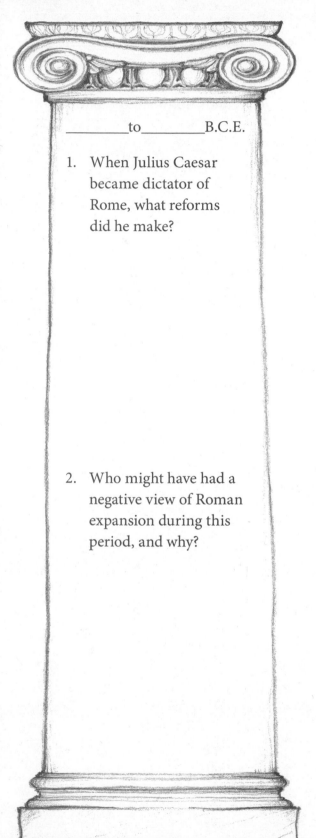

_____to_____B.C.E.

1. When Julius Caesar became dictator of Rome, what reforms did he make?

2. Who might have had a negative view of Roman expansion during this period, and why?

Section 5

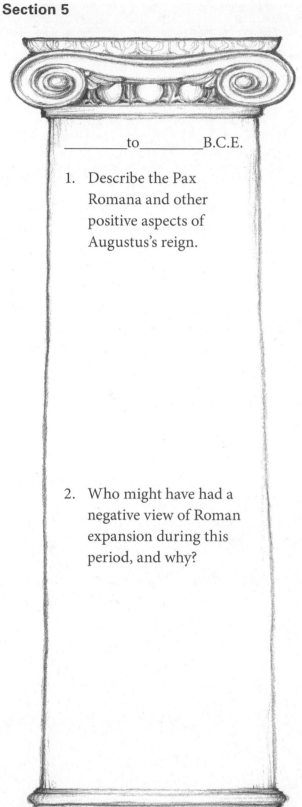

_____to_____B.C.E.

1. Describe the Pax Romana and other positive aspects of Augustus's reign.

2. Who might have had a negative view of Roman expansion during this period, and why?

In the T-chart below, list at least three benefits and at least three costs of Roman expansion from 509 B.C.E. to 14 C.E.

Benefits of Roman Expansion	Costs of Roman Expansion

In a well-written paragraph, explain whether you think the benefits of Roman expansion outweighed the costs. Support your opinion by giving specific evidence from your T-chart and from the lesson.

© Teachers' Curriculum Institute

Daily Life in the Roman Empire

How did wealth affect daily life in the Roman Empire?

The statements below describe daily life in the Roman Empire. For each statement, circle whether you think it describes the life of a rich Roman or of a poor Roman.

Aspect of Daily Life	Statement	My Prediction	
Law and Order	Faced more severe punishment for breaking the law.	rich	poor
Religion	Celebrated religious festivals and holidays.	rich	poor
Family Life	Women ran the household and trained slaves.	rich	poor
Food and Drink	Ate meat, bread, parrots, and jellyfish for dinner.	rich	poor
Housing	Lived in small apartments that were crowded, noisy, and dirty.	rich	poor
Education	Learned math, science, literature, and music.	rich	poor
Recreation	Attended plays and sat on cushions at the Circus Maximus.	rich	poor
Country Life	In the countryside, worked on farms and lived in huts.	rich	poor

What questions do you have about life in the Roman Empire? Record at least two questions in the space below.

READING NOTES

Social Studies Vocabulary

As you complete the Reading Notes, use these terms in your answers.

Forum   paterfamilias   Circus Maximus
rule of law   Colosseum

Section 1

List two ways that life differed for rich and poor people of the Roman Empire.

Rich Romans	Poor Romans
•	•
•	•

Section 2

Complete the Venn diagram below by describing *law and order* in the Roman Empire.

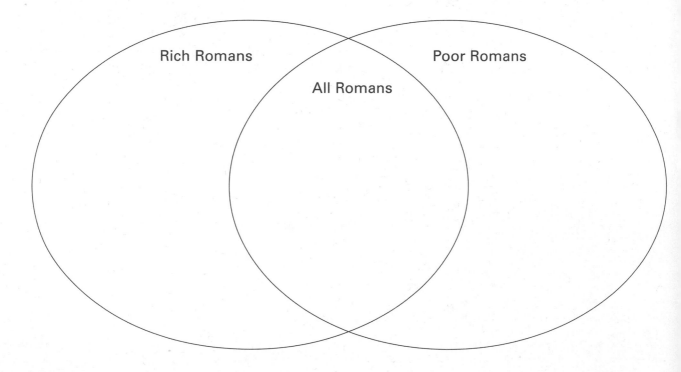

Rich Romans   All Romans   Poor Romans

© Teachers' Curriculum Institute

Section 3

Complete the Venn diagram below by describing *religion* in the Roman Empire.

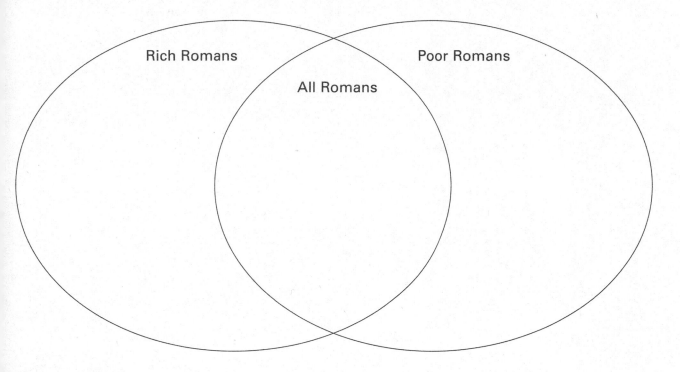

Section 4

Complete the Venn diagram below by describing *family life* in the Roman Empire.

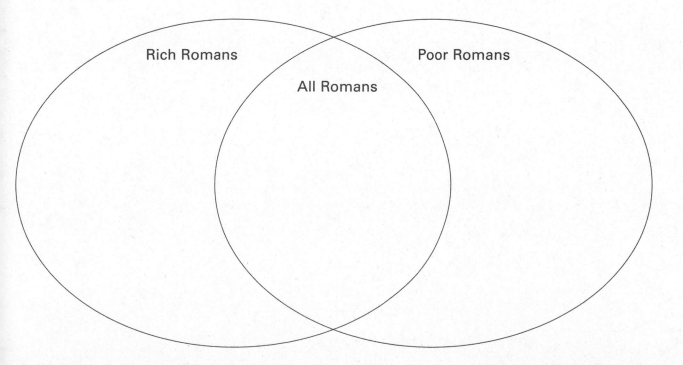

Section 5

Complete the Venn diagram below by describing *food and drink* in the Roman Empire.

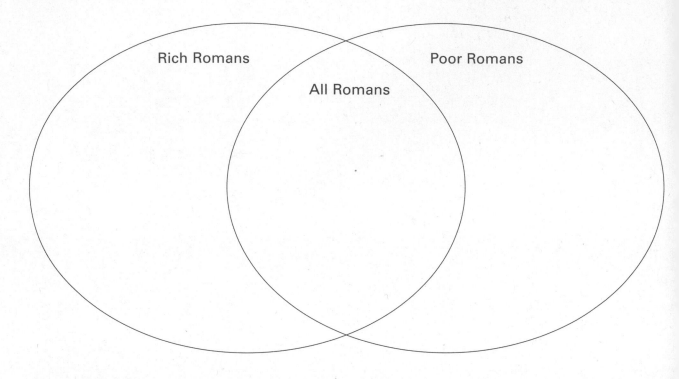

Section 6

Complete the Venn diagram below by describing *housing* in the Roman Empire.

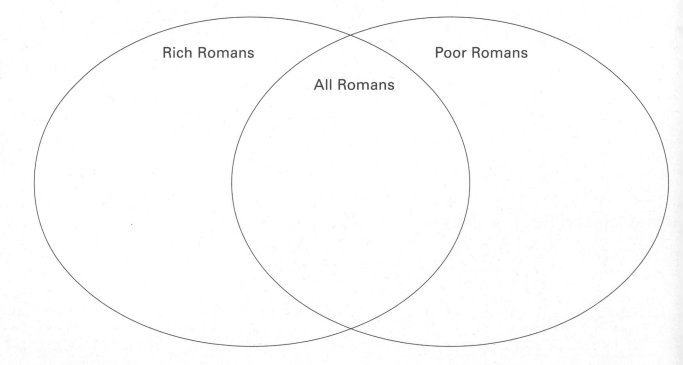

© Teachers' Curriculum Institute

Complete the Venn diagram below by describing *education* in the Roman Empire.

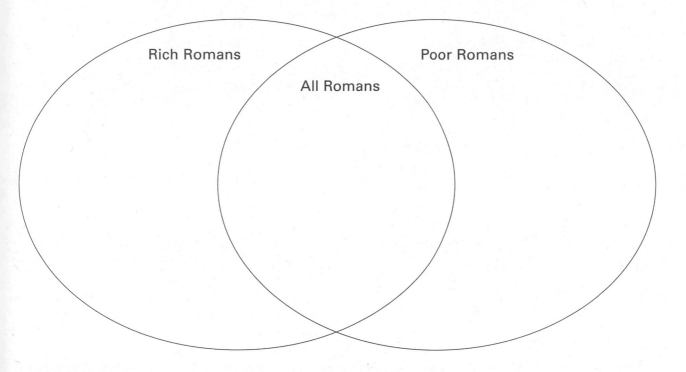

Complete the Venn diagram below by describing *recreation* in the Roman Empire.

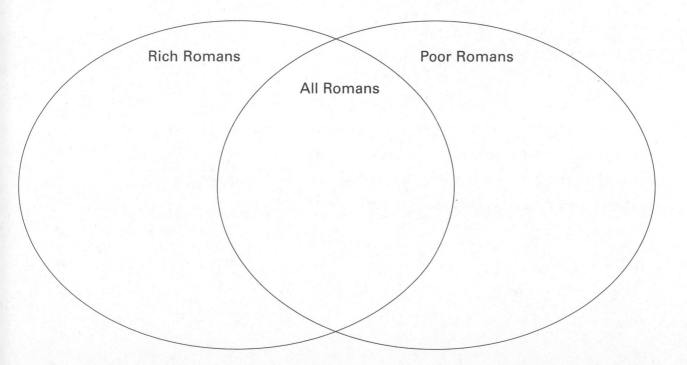

Complete the Venn diagram below by describing *country life* in the Roman Empire.

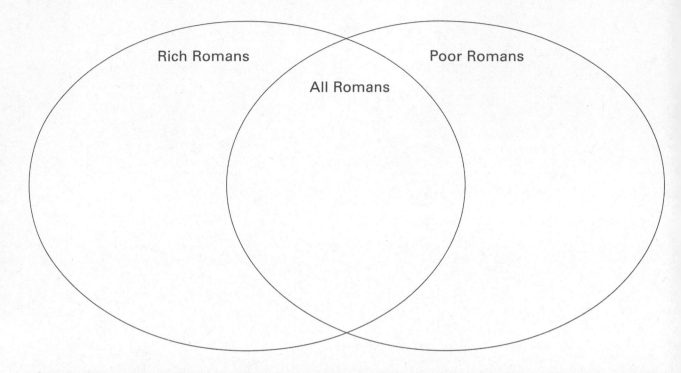

Rich Romans

All Romans

Poor Romans

PROCESSING

On a separate piece of paper, write a dialogue between a rich Roman and a poor Roman that might have taken place in 100 C.E. Your dialogue must

- be written as if two people were talking to each other.
- begin with these opening lines:

  Rich Roman: "Life is great in the Roman Empire!"

  Poor Roman: "Not for all of us! What's so good about your daily life?"

  Rich Roman: "Rome is an amazing place if you have money. For example, . . ."

- describe at least four aspects of life from a rich Roman's perspective.
- describe at least four aspects of life from a poor Roman's perspective.
- be free of spelling and grammatical errors.

© Teachers' Curriculum Institute

INVESTIGATING PRIMARY SOURCES

Using Questions and Evaluating Sources

Think about what you know about Roman gladiators. What else do you want to learn about this group? List some questions you have about gladiators.

Question 1:

Question 2:

Question 3:

Read Investigating Primary Sources, Were Gladiators Heroes?, in the Student Text. Use the primary sources in the reading and reliable sources from the Internet or books to answer the questions. For each source, consider if it helps answer the question and why it was created.

Answer 1:

Source:

Answer 2:

Source:

Answer 3:

Source:

Use the evidence you gathered to make a claim to this question: *Were gladiators heroes?*

Claim:

Constructing an Argument

Create an argument to answer the question: *Were gladiators heroes?* Your argument should:

- clearly state your claim.
- include evidence from multiple sources.
- provide explanations for how the sources support the claim.

Use this rubric to evaluate your argument. Make changes as needed.

Score	Description
3	The claim clearly answers the question. The argument uses evidence from two or more primary sources that strongly support the claim. The explanations accurately connect to the evidence and claim.
2	The claim answers the question. The argument uses evidence from one or more primary sources that support the claim. Some of the explanations connect to the evidence and claim.
1	The claim fails to answer the question. The argument lacks evidence from primary sources. Explanations are missing or are unrelated to the evidence and claim.

© Teachers' Curriculum Institute

The Origins and Spread of Christianity

How did Christianity originate and spread?

Aesop's Fables is a collection of brief stories said to have been written by a Greek slave named Aesop, who may have lived from 620 to 560 B.C.E. A fable is a short story that teaches a moral lesson. Follow along on Handout A as your teacher plays "The Lion and the Mouse" fable. Then follow the directions and answer the questions below.

1. List the characters in the fable.

2. Summarize the plot.

3. What moral lesson do you think this fable is trying to teach?

4. Do you think this kind of storytelling is effective? Why or why not?

READING NOTES

Social Studies Vocabulary

As you complete the Reading Notes, use these terms in your answers.

Christianity	Gospel	Resurrection
Jesus	disciple	missionary
Messiah	parable	Constantine

Section 1

1. Where was Judea and why was it important to the Jews?

2. For each date on the timeline below, describe how the Romans ruled Judea and how Jews reacted to Roman rule.

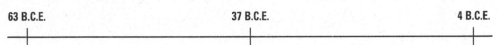

63 B.C.E.   37 B.C.E.   4 B.C.E.

Section 2

1. What are the Gospels and who wrote them?

2. Describe Jesus's birth according to the Gospels.

     © Teachers' Curriculum Institute

1. According to the Gospels, what did Jesus say were the two most important of all the Jewish laws?

   •

   •

2. Summarize the Parable of the Good Samaritan and explain its moral lesson.

Summary of the Parable of the Good Samaritan	Moral Lesson of the Parable of the Good Samaritan

3. According to the Gospels, why was Jesus condemned to die on a cross?

4. Why was belief in the Resurrection important to Jesus's disciples and other Christians?

Section 4

1. What caused Paul to stop persecuting Christians and become a missionary?

2. How did Paul's work help to spread Christianity?

Section 5

1. Why were Christians considered a threat to Rome?

2. Complete the following flowchart about the Roman persecution of Christians.

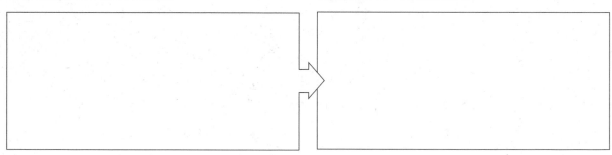

Methods of Persecution   Results of Persecution

3. Describe the role of Constantine, and Roman emperors who followed him, in spreading Christianity.

© Teachers' Curriculum Institute

PROCESSING

As you have learned, a parable is a brief story that teaches a moral lesson. In the space below, write your own parable that teaches a lesson about some aspect of good citizenship. For example, it might be about the importance of voting or of volunteering in your community. Include a symbol or small illustration that shows the main idea of the moral lesson you want to teach.

Learning About World Religions: Christianity

How are Christians' lives shaped by the beliefs and practices of Christianity?

PREVIEW

On the left side of the T-chart, list at least three things you may already know about Christianity. On the right side of the chart, list at least three questions about Christianity that you want to know the answers to.

Already Know	Want to Know

READING NOTES

Social Studies Vocabulary

As you complete the Reading Notes, use these terms in your answers.

Trinity	Eastern Orthodox Church	baptism
salvation	Protestant	Holy Communion
Roman Catholic Church	sacrament	

Complete the spoke diagram below by listing each of the central beliefs of Christianity. Then write a sentence or some phrases to describe each one.

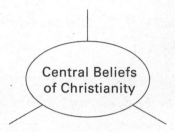

1. How did the Roman Catholic Church and the Eastern Orthodox Church become separate?

2. Who was Martin Luther and what is he famous for?

3. What was the main result of the Reformation?

© Teachers' Curriculum Institute

Section 3

1. What is a sacrament?

2. What happens during a baptism and what does it mean?

3. What is Holy Communion, and what does it symbolize?

Section 4

1. What do Christian church buildings have in common? In what ways can they differ?

2. Why do many Christian groups attend services on Sundays?

On the timeline below, arrange the following holidays in the correct order to show, roughly, when they occur each year: Palm Sunday, Lent, Good Friday, Easter, and Christmas. Then add a caption that tells the main purpose of each one.

| December | January | March | April |

PROCESSING

Look at the right side of the T-chart in the Preview activity. Choose one question that was answered during this lesson. Write the question and the answer here.

Then, in the space below, explain three important ways that Christians' lives are shaped by their beliefs and practices.

© Teachers' Curriculum Institute

The Legacy of Rome in the Modern World

To what extent does ancient Rome influence us today?

How much do you think ancient Rome influences modern culture? For each statement in the matrix below, circle the level of influence you think exists today for that aspect of Roman culture. If you can, give a specific example to support your opinion.

Aspect of Culture	Extent of Influence	Supporting Example
Roman art influences us today.	Not at All Barely Moderately Greatly	
Roman architecture and engineering influence us today.	Not at All Barely Moderately Greatly	
Roman language influences us today.	Not at All Barely Moderately Greatly	
Roman philosophy and law influence us today.	Not at All Barely Moderately Greatly	

READING NOTES

Social Studies Vocabulary

As you complete the Reading Notes, use these terms in your answers.

Byzantine Empire   Renaissance   aqueduct   Stoicism
patron   triumphal arch   Latin   natural law

Section 1

After reading Section 1, complete the following tasks:

1. On each "crack" in the arch below, write one of the problems that caused the Roman Empire to decline and fall. One has been done for you. Then draw a symbol or illustration to represent the problem.

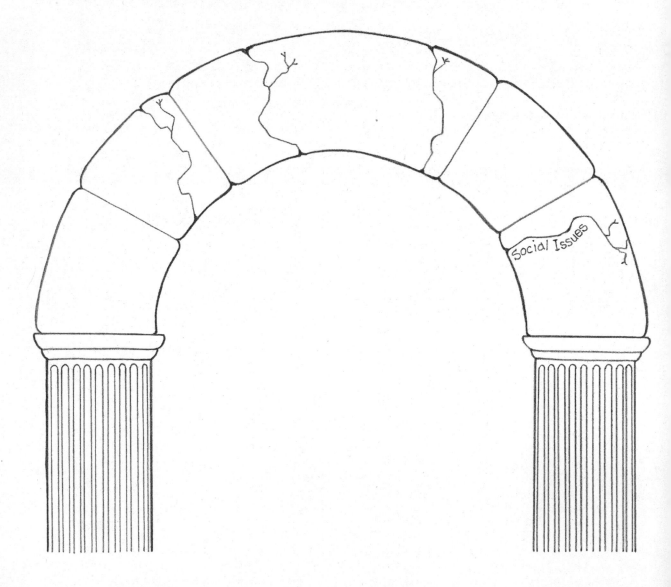

© Teachers' Curriculum Institute

2. For each date below, describe the event that led to the collapse of the western Roman Empire.

	117 C.E.	Height of the Roman Empire
	330 C.E.	
	410 C.E.	
	476 C.E.	

3. On the map below, follow these steps to show what became of the eastern Roman Empire.

   - Label the city of Rome.

   - Draw an arrow from Rome to the new city that Emperor Constantine made his capital, Constantinople. Label it.

   - Color and label the Byzantine Empire.

The Remains of the Roman Empire, About 500 C.E.

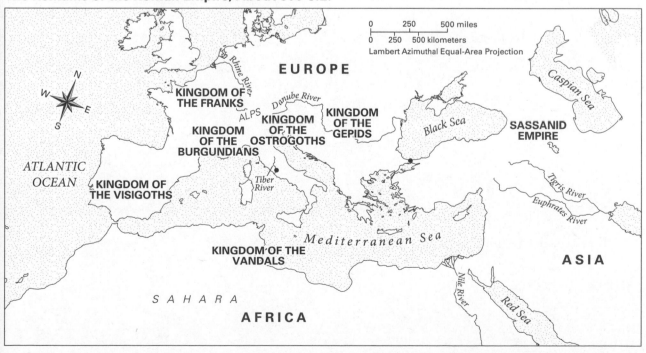

After reading each of Sections 2 to 5, answer the corresponding questions in complete sentences.

Section 2

1. Choose four types of Roman art that interest you. Write a short description of each type.

   •

   •

   •

   •

2. What are some examples of how Roman art influences us today?

© Teachers' Curriculum Institute

Section 3

1. Choose four Roman architectural and engineering achievements that impress you most. Write a short description of each achievement.

    •

    •

    •

    •

2. What are some examples of how Roman architecture and engineering influence us today?

Section 4

1. How was the Latin alphabet of Rome different from the English alphabet today?

2. What Roman numerals are used for the numbers 1 through 10? How were the numbers 50, 100, 500, and 1,000 written by the Romans?

3. List some examples of how Roman language influences us today.

Section 5

1. Describe the three most important ideas in Roman philosophy and law.

    •

    •

    •

2. What are some examples of how Roman philosophy and law influence us today?

PROCESSING

To what extent do Roman achievements affect your community today—not at all, barely, moderately, or greatly? *On a separate sheet of paper,* write a strong thesis statement answering this question. Then list at least three pieces of evidence that support your thesis statement.

© Teachers' Curriculum Institute

Preparing to Write: Being an Urban Planner

Urban planners who studied Pompeii asked themselves several questions that could apply to cities and towns in the United States today:

- Are there public spaces where people can gather?
- Do the buildings serve the needs of the people who live and work in them? Do the buildings look as though they belong together?
- Is it convenient for people and vehicles to move around the city?

Think of two more questions that would help you determine whether you would find a city "livable."

Example: Are there playgrounds and sports facilities for young people?

1.

2.

Is Your Town or City Well Planned?

Use the planners' questions and your own questions to think about whether your town or city is well planned. Write down which features show good urban planning and which do not.

Good Planning	Poor Planning

Writing a Business Letter

Write a letter to your municipal planning commission. Introduce yourself as a resident of your community. Tell your officials why some features of your city or town show good planning. Then suggest how other features could be improved. Use the ideas on the previous page to guide you in writing your letter. Organize your letter in a way that presents your ideas clearly. Use good paragraph and sentence structure.

Use this rubric to evaluate your letter. Make changes to your work if you need to.

Score	Description
3	Relevant examples of good and poor planning are provided. Suggestions for improvement are included. There are no spelling or grammar errors.
2	Somewhat relevant examples of good and poor planning are provided. Some suggestions for improvement are included. There are some spelling or grammar errors.
1	Few or no relevant examples of good and poor planning are provided. Few or no suggestions for improvement are included. There are many spelling or grammar errors.

© Teachers' Curriculum Institute

Timeline Skills

Analyze the Unit 6 timeline in the Student Text. Also think about what you have learned in this unit. Then answer the following questions.

1. About how long after Rome was founded was the Roman Republic formed?

2. How was the Roman Republic created?

3. For about how many years did the plebeians rebel against patrician rule? What was accomplished?

4. Did Rome conquer Italy before or after it conquered Carthage?

5. When were the Punic Wars fought?

6. Of Julius Caesar, Augustus, and Constantine, who was the last to rule Rome?

7. During whose rule did the Pax Romana happen?

8. According to the timeline, who helped spread Christianity, and how did he do it?

9. When did Rome allow Christians the freedom to openly worship?

10. About how many miles of roads did Roman workers construct?

© Teachers' Curriculum Institute

Critical Thinking

Use the timeline and the lessons in the unit to answer the following questions.

11. What were the main features of the Roman Republic, and how did they change over time?

12. Today, Christianity is a major world religion. Describe two events that helped spread Christianity during Roman times.

13. Which contribution do you think is Rome's greatest legacy, and why?

14. If you could add three more events to this timeline, which ones would you choose? List each event and explain why you think it is important enough to add to the timeline.

    a.

    b.

    c.

© Teachers' Curriculum Institute

Cover and Title Page:
Christian Delbert/Dreamstime

Lesson 1
7T: Arindam Banerjee/Dreamstime
7B: Hemis/Alamy **8T:** Shutterstock
8B: Werner Forman / Art Resource, NY
9T: Universal History Archive/Getty Images
9B: De Agostini Picture Library / A. Dagli Orti /
Bridgeman Images

Lesson 2
12T: Sabena Jane Blackbird/Alamy
13T: Markus Schieder/Dreamstime
14T: Markus Schieder/Dreamstime
15T: Markus Schieder/Dreamstime

Lesson 4
29: Gualberto Becerra/ Shutterstock

Lesson 14
105: National Museum of India, New Delhi, India /
Bridgeman Images

Lesson 16
118: British Library, London, UK / © British Library
Board. All Rights Reserved / Bridgeman Images
119T: British Library, London, UK / © British Library
Board. All Rights Reserved / Bridgeman Images
119B: Shutterstock
120T: Shutterstock
120B: Alfredo Dagli Orti / The Art Archive at Art
Resource, NY

Lesson 22
160T: Bibliotheque Nationale, Paris, France / Archives
Charmet / Bridgeman Images
161TL: Blue Jean Images/Corbis
161TR: Sovfoto/Getty Images
162T: Granger, NYC
163T: Granger, NYC

Lesson 32
223L: Lanmas/Alamy
223R: Granger, NYC